Easy Does It...

Good Housekeeping

Easy Does It...

PAVILION

First published in the United Kingdom in 2014 by
Pavilion Books Company Limited
1 Gower Street
London
WC1E 6HD

The Good Housekeeping website is
www.goodhousekeeping.co.uk

10 9 8 7 6 5 4 3 2 1

ISBN 978-1-910231-03-6

A catalogue record for this book is available from the British Library.

Reproduction by Dot Gradations Ltd, UK
Printed and bound by Times Offset (M) Sdn Bhd, Malaysia

This book can be ordered direct from the publisher at www.pavilionbooks.com

Picture Credits:
Photographers: Neil Barclay (pages 15, 20,
54, 71, 76, 77, 82, 88, 96, 98, 99, 101,
137, 172 and 190); Martin Brigdale (pages
115, 118, 119, 138, 139, 144, 145, 152,
173, 177, 182, 198, 200, 201, 204, 227
and 228); Nicki Dowey (pages 8, 9, 10, 11,
12, 13, 14, 16, 17, 18, 19, 21, 22, 23, 24,
26, 27, 28, 29, 32, 34, 35, 37, 39, 40, 41,
42, 43, 44, 46, 49, 50, 51, 52, 53, 59, 63,
65, 66, 67, 69, 72, 73, 74, 78, 83, 84, 85,
90, 91, 95, 97, 100, 103, 104, 107, 108,
116, 122, 123, 124, 126, 130, 131, 134,
135, 136, 140, 142, 147, 149, 153, 156,
157, 159, 160, 161, 162, 163, 165, 169,
170, 171, 175, 176, 178, 181, 183, 185,
188, 193, 195, 199, 202, 203, 205, 207,
208, 209, 210, 211, 217, 220, 223, 230,
235, 236 and 237); Will Heap (pages 25,
58, 125, 166, 189, 212 and 218); Gareth
Morgans (page 155); Craig Robertson
(pages 36, 47, 48, 57, 62, 64, 70, 75, 79,
80, 81, 89, 93, 102, 103, 105, 109, 111,
112, 117, 127, 129, 133, 141, 143, 146,
167, 174, 176, 180, 191, 192, 197, 221,
213, 216, 219, 221, 222, 224, 225, 229,
231, 232, 233 and 234); Lucinda Symons
(pages 33, 45, 55, 60, 67, 68, 70, 106, 113,
158, 179, 194 and 196).

Home Economists: Anna Burges-Lumsden,
Joanna Farrow, Emma Jane Frost, Teresa
Goldfinch, Alice Hart, Lucy McKelvie, Mari
Mererid Williams, Kim Morphew, Katie
Rogers, Bridget Sargeson and Jennifer
White.

Stylists: Susannah Blake, Wei Tang, Helen
Trent and Fanny Ward.

Notes
Both metric and imperial measures are given for the recipes. Follow either set of measures,
not a mixture of both, as they are not interchangeable.
All spoon measures are level.
1 tsp = 5ml spoon; 1 tbsp = 15ml spoon.
Ovens and grills must be preheated to the specified temperature.
Medium eggs should be used except where otherwise specified.

Dietary Guidelines
Note that certain recipes contain raw or lightly cooked eggs. The young, elderly, pregnant
women and anyone with immune-deficiency disease should avoid these because of the slight
risk of salmonella.
Note that some recipes contain alcohol. Check the ingredients list before serving to children.

Contents

START THE DAY

Porridge with Dried Fruit

Preparation Time 5 minutes • Cooking Time 5 minutes • Serves 4 • Per Serving 279 calories,
6g fat (of which 1g saturates), 49g carbohydrate, 0.2g salt • Vegetarian • Easy

200g (7oz) porridge oats
400ml (14fl oz) milk, plus extra
** to serve**
75g (3oz) mixture of chopped dried
** figs, apricots and raisins**

1. Put the oats into a large pan and add the milk and 400ml (14fl oz) water. Stir in the figs, apricots and raisins and heat gently, stirring until the porridge thickens and the oats are cooked.

2. Divide among four bowls and serve with a splash of milk.

Toasted Oats with Berries

Preparation Time 10 minutes, plus cooling • Cooking Time 5–10 minutes • Serves 4 • Per Serving 327 calories, 15g fat (of which 3g saturates), 44g carbohydrate, 0.1g salt • Vegetarian • Easy

25g (1oz) hazelnuts, roughly chopped
125g (4oz) rolled oats
1 tbsp olive oil
125g (4oz) strawberries, sliced
250g (9oz) blueberries
200g (7oz) Greek yogurt
2 tbsp runny honey

1. Preheat the grill to medium. Put the hazelnuts into a bowl with the oats. Drizzle with the oil and mix well, then spread out on a baking sheet. Toast the oat mixture for 5–10 minutes until it starts to crisp up. Remove from the heat and set aside to cool.

2. Put the strawberries into a large bowl with the blueberries and yogurt. Stir in the oats and hazelnuts, drizzle with the honey and divide among four dishes. Serve immediately.

COOK'S TIP
Blueberries contain a substance that helps the gut to stay clean and healthy, and, like cranberries, they are rich in antioxidants.

TRY SOMETHING DIFFERENT
Use a mixture of raspberries, blackberries, or chopped nectarines or peaches instead of the strawberries and blueberries.

Energy-boosting Muesli

Preparation Time 5 minutes • Makes 15 servings • Per Serving 208 calories, 9g fat (of which trace saturates), 28g carbohydrate, 0g salt • Vegetarian • Easy

500g (1lb 2oz) porridge oats
100g (3½oz) toasted almonds,
**   chopped**
2 tbsp pumpkin seeds
2 tbsp sunflower seeds
100g (3½oz) ready-to-eat dried
**   apricots, chopped**
milk or yogurt to serve

1. Mix the oats with the almonds, seeds and apricots. Store in a sealable container: it will keep for up to one month. Serve with milk or yogurt.

COOK'S TIP
Oats contain gluten and, strictly speaking, are not suitable for coeliacs. However, because they contain a much smaller amount than wheat, rye or barley, research shows that most people with coeliac disease can safely eat moderate amounts. The oats must be from a source where there is no risk of contamination from wheat or wheat products during processing or packing. As individual tolerance to gluten varies, if you are a coeliac, seek expert advice before eating oats.

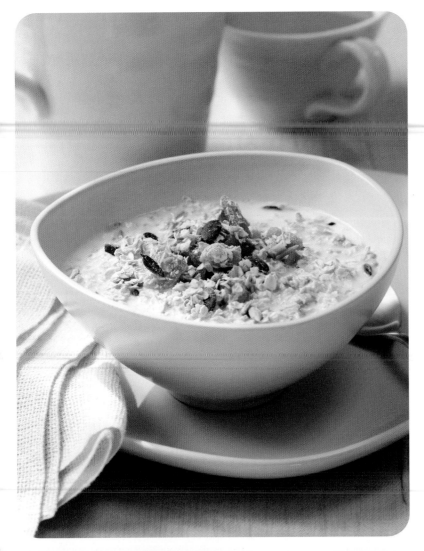

Classic French Omelette

Preparation Time 5 minutes • Cooking Time 5 minutes • Serves 1 • Per Serving 449 calories, 40g fat (of which 19g saturates), 1g carbohydrate, 1g salt • Vegetarian • Easy

2–3 medium eggs
1 tbsp milk or water
25g (1oz) unsalted butter
salt and ground black pepper
sliced or grilled tomatoes and
  freshly chopped flat-leafed
  parsley to serve

1. Whisk the eggs in a bowl, just enough to break them down – over-beating spoils the texture of the omelette. Season with salt and pepper and add the milk or water.

2. Heat the butter in an 18cm (7in) omelette pan or non-stick frying pan until it is foaming, but not brown. Add the eggs and stir gently with a fork or wooden spatula, drawing the mixture from the sides to the centre as it sets and letting the liquid egg in the centre run to the sides. When set, stop stirring and cook for 30 seconds or until the omelette is golden brown underneath and still creamy on top: don't overcook. If you are making a filled omelette (see Try Something Different), add the filling at this point.

3. Tilt the pan away from you slightly and use a palette knife to fold over one-third of the omelette to the centre, then fold over the opposite third. Slide the omelette out on to a warmed plate, letting it flip over so that the folded sides are underneath. Serve immediately, with tomatoes sprinkled with parsley.

TRY SOMETHING DIFFERENT
• *Blend 25g (1oz) mild goat's cheese with 1 tbsp crème fraîche; put in the centre of the omelette before folding.*
• *Toss 25g (1oz) chopped smoked salmon or cooked smoked haddock with a little chopped dill and 1 tbsp crème fraîche; scatter over the omelette before folding.*

Creamy Baked Eggs

Preparation Time 5 minutes • Cooking Time 15–18 minutes • Serves 4 • Per Serving 153 calories,
14g fat (of which 7g saturates), 1g carbohydrate, 0.2g salt • Vegetarian • Easy

butter to grease
4 sun-dried tomatoes
4 medium eggs
4 tbsp double cream
salt and ground black pepper
Granary bread to serve (optional)

1. Preheat the oven to 180°C (160°C fan oven) mark 4. Grease four individual ramekins.

2. Put a tomato into each ramekin and season to taste with salt and pepper. Carefully break an egg on top of each tomato, then drizzle 1 tbsp cream over each egg.

3. Bake for 15–18 minutes – the eggs will continue to cook once they have been taken out of the oven.

4. Leave to stand for 2 minutes before serving. Serve with Granary bread, if you like.

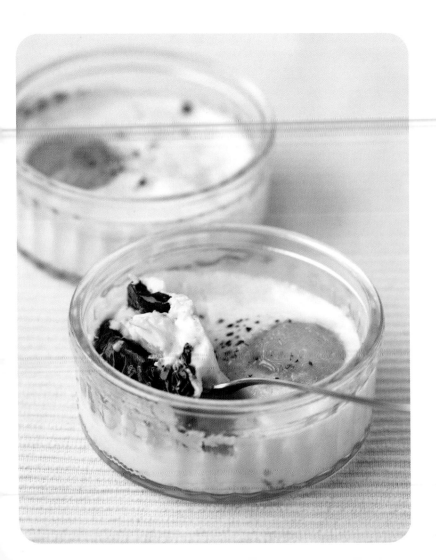

Piperade

Preparation Time 20 minutes • Cooking Time 20 minutes • Serves 4 • Per Serving 232 calories, 17g fat (of which 4g saturates), 7g carbohydrate, 0.4g salt • Vegetarian • Easy

2 tbsp olive oil
1 medium onion, finely chopped
1 garlic clove, finely chopped
1 red pepper, seeded and chopped
375g (13oz) tomatoes, peeled,
seeded and chopped
a pinch of cayenne pepper
8 large eggs
salt and ground black pepper
freshly chopped flat-leafed parsley
to garnish
fresh bread to serve (optional)

1. Heat the oil in a heavy-based frying pan. Add the onion and cook gently for 5 minutes. Add the red pepper and cook for 10 minutes or until softened.

2. Add the tomatoes, increase the heat and cook until they are reduced to a thick pulp. Season well with cayenne pepper, salt and pepper.

3. Lightly whisk the eggs and add to the frying pan. Using a wooden spoon, stir gently until they've just begun to set but are still creamy. Garnish with parsley and serve with bread, if you like.

Poached Eggs with Mushrooms

Preparation Time 15 minutes • Cooking Time 20 minutes • Serves 4 • Per Serving 276 calories,
23g fat (of which 9g saturates), 1g carbohydrate, 0.7g salt • Vegetarian • Easy

**8 medium-sized flat or portabella
    mushrooms**
40g (1½oz) butter
8 medium eggs
225g (8oz) baby spinach leaves
4 tsp fresh pesto

1. Preheat the oven to 200°C (180°C fan oven) mark 6. Arrange the mushrooms in a single layer in a small roasting tin and dot with the butter. Roast for 15 minutes or until golden brown and soft.

2. Meanwhile, bring a wide shallow pan of water to the boil. When the mushrooms are half-cooked and the water is bubbling furiously, break the eggs into the pan, spaced well apart, then take the pan off the heat. The eggs will take about 6 minutes to cook.

3. When the mushrooms are tender, put them on a warmed plate, cover and return to the turned-off oven to keep warm.

4. Put the roasting tin over a medium heat on the hob and add the spinach. Cook, stirring, for about 30 seconds or until the spinach has just started to wilt.

5. The eggs should be set by now, so divide the mushrooms among four warmed plates and top with a little spinach, a poached egg and a teaspoonful of pesto.

**TRY SOMETHING
DIFFERENT**
*For a more substantial meal,
serve on 100% rye bread or
German pumpernickel.*

Scrambled Eggs with Smoked Salmon

Preparation Time 10 minutes • Cooking Time 5 minutes • Serves 4 • Per Serving 457 calories, 34g fat (of which 17g saturates), 17g carbohydrate, 2.7g salt • Easy

6 large eggs
25g (1oz) butter, plus extra to spread
100g (3½oz) mascarpone cheese
125g pack smoked salmon, sliced, or smoked salmon trimmings
6 slices sourdough or rye bread, toasted, buttered and cut into slim rectangles for soldiers
salt and ground black pepper

1. Crack the eggs into a jug and lightly beat together. Season well.

2. Melt the butter in a non-stick pan over a low heat. Add the eggs and stir constantly until the mixture thickens. Add the mascarpone and season well. Cook for 1–2 minutes longer, until the mixture just becomes firm, then fold in the smoked salmon. Serve at once with toasted bread soldiers.

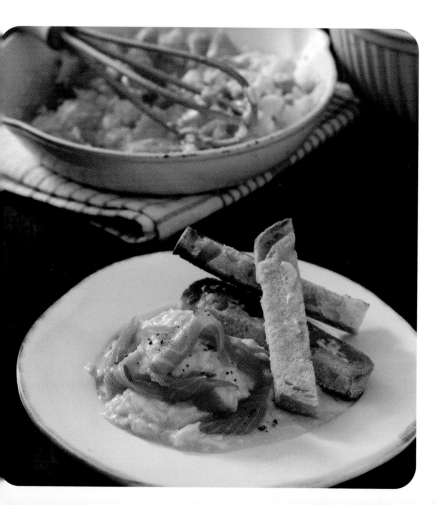

Beans on Toast

Preparation Time 5 minutes • Cooking Time 10 minutes • Serves 4 • Per Serving 364 calories,
9g fat (of which 2g saturates), 55g carbohydrate, 2.1g salt • Easy

1 tbsp olive oil
2 garlic cloves, finely sliced
400g can borlotti or cannellini
 beans, drained and rinsed
400g can chickpeas
400g can chopped tomatoes
leaves from 2 fresh rosemary
 sprigs, finely chopped
4 thick slices Granary bread
25g (1oz) Parmesan
chopped fresh parsley to serve

1. Heat the oil in a pan over a low heat, add the garlic and cook for 1 minute, stirring gently.

2. Add the beans and chickpeas to the pan with the tomatoes and bring to the boil. Add the rosemary, then reduce the heat and simmer for 8–10 minutes until thickened.

3. Meanwhile, toast the bread and put on to plates. Grate the Parmesan into the bean mixture, stir once, then spoon over the bread. Serve immediately, scattered with parsley.

TRY SOMETHING DIFFERENT
This will be just as good with toasted soda bread or seeded bread, mixed beans instead of borlotti or cannellini, and grated Gruyère cheese or Cheddar instead of Parmesan.

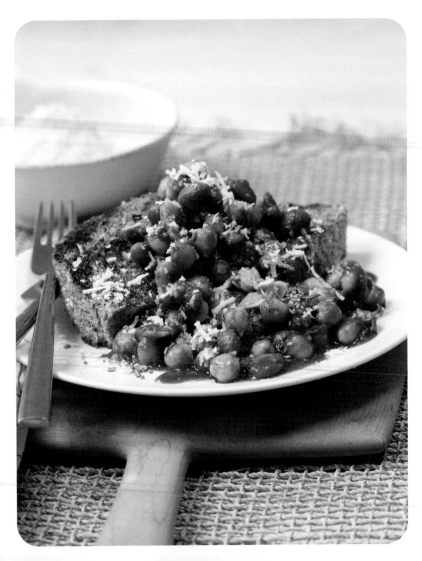

BLT-topped Bagels with Hollandaise Sauce

Preparation Time 15 minutes • Cooking Time 8 minutes • Serves 6 • Per Serving 384 calories, 31g fat (of which 16g saturates), 16g carbohydrate, 1.9g salt • Easy

3 large bagels, cut in half
   horizontally
25g (1oz) butter, softened
12 smoked streaky bacon rashers,
   rind removed
2 tsp olive oil
3 tomatoes, cut into thick slices

150ml (¼ pint) bought Hollandaise
   Sauce (or make your own, see
   page 59)
75g (3oz) rocket leaves
crushed black pepper to garnish

1. Preheat the grill to high, then grill the halved bagels until golden. Spread generously with the butter. Cover the bagels with a piece of foil and keep them warm. Grill the bacon for 2–3 minutes until crisp, then keep warm. Heat the oil in a small frying pan until very hot and fry the tomatoes for about 1 minute until lightly charred.

2. Put the hollandaise sauce in a small pan and heat gently. To assemble, top the warm bagels with a few rocket leaves, the tomatoes and bacon. Spoon the warm hollandaise sauce over the bacon and garnish with the pepper. Serve at once.

Boxty Pancakes

Preparation Time 20 minutes • Cooking Time 30 minutes • Serves 6 • Per Serving 340 calories, 19g fat (of which 7g saturates), 29g carbohydrate, 2g salt • Easy

450g (1lb) floury potatoes, such as
   Maris Piper
75g (3oz) plain flour
1 tsp baking powder
150ml (¼ pint) buttermilk
4 medium eggs
2 tbsp sunflower oil
4 large rashers unsmoked bacon
15g (½oz) butter
200g (7oz) black pudding, chopped
150g (5oz) cherry tomatoes, halved

2 tbsp red wine vinegar
50ml (2fl oz) vegetable stock
2 tbsp each freshly chopped chives
   and oregano
salt and ground black pepper

1. Chop half the potatoes and put into a pan of cold water. Bring to the boil, then reduce the heat and simmer for 15–20 minutes. Mash and set aside.

2. Sift the flour, baking powder and 1½ tsp salt into a large bowl. Grate the remaining potato, then wrap in a clean teatowel and squeeze out all the moisture. Add it to the dry ingredients with the mash. Season with pepper and stir well. Mix together the buttermilk and eggs, then stir into the potato mixture.

3. Preheat the oven to 180°C (160°C fan oven) mark 4. Heat the oil in an ovenproof 23–25.5cm (9–10in) non-stick ovenproof frying pan and pour in the potato mixture. Flatten the top and turn the heat to low. Cook gently for 10 minutes or until golden underneath. Cover the pan with a plate, tip the pancake on to the plate, then slide the pancake back into the pan and cook the other side for 5 minutes. Transfer the pan to the oven and cook for 10 minutes.

4. Meanwhile, fry the bacon, slice thickly and keep warm. In the same pan, melt the butter and add the black pudding. Fry for 5 minutes, then stir in the cherry tomatoes, vinegar and stock and cook for 1 minute. Take off the heat and add most of the herbs, then season and set aside.

5. When the pancake is ready, put on to a board and slice into six. Put each slice on a plate and spoon some of the black pudding and bacon mixture over each pancake. Garnish with the remaining herbs and serve.

Lemon & Blueberry Pancakes

Preparation Time 15 minutes • Cooking Time 10–15 minutes • Serves 4 • Per Serving 290 calories, 13g fat (of which 6g saturates), 39g carbohydrate, 0.6g salt • Vegetarian • Easy

125g (4oz) wholemeal plain flour
1 tsp baking powder
¼ tsp bicarbonate of soda
2 tbsp golden caster sugar
finely grated zest of 1 lemon
125g (4oz) natural yogurt
2 tbsp milk

2 medium eggs
40g (1½oz) butter
100g (3½oz) blueberries
1 tsp sunflower oil
natural yogurt and fruit compote
   to serve

1. Sift the flour, baking powder and bicarbonate of soda into a bowl, tipping in the contents left in the sieve. Add the sugar and lemon zest. Pour in the yogurt and milk. Break the eggs into the mixture and whisk together.

2. Melt 25g (1oz) butter in a pan, add to the bowl with the blueberries and stir everything together.

3. Heat a dot of butter with the oil in a frying pan over a medium heat until hot. Add four large spoonfuls of the mixture to the pan to make four pancakes. After about 2 minutes, flip them over and cook for 1–2 minutes. Repeat with the remaining mixture, adding a dot more butter each time.

4. Serve with natural yogurt and some fruit compote.

TRY SOMETHING DIFFERENT
Instead of blueberries and lemon, use 100g (3½oz) chopped ready-to-eat dried apricots and 2 tsp grated fresh root ginger.

French Toast

Preparation Time 5 minutes • Cooking Time 10 minutes • Serves 4 • Per Finger 259 calories,
20g fat (of which 9g saturates), 15g carbohydrate, 0.7g salt • Vegetarian • Easy

2 medium eggs
150ml (¼ pint) semi-skimmed milk
a generous pinch of freshly grated
  nutmeg or ground cinnamon
4 slices white bread, or fruit bread,
  crusts removed and each slice
  cut into four fingers

50g (2oz) butter
vegetable oil for frying
1 tbsp golden caster sugar

1. Put the eggs, milk and nutmeg or cinnamon into a shallow dish and beat together.

2. Dip the pieces of bread into the mixture, coating them well.

3. Heat half the butter with 1 tbsp oil in a heavy-based frying pan. When the butter is foaming, fry the egg-coated bread pieces in batches, until golden on both sides, adding more butter and oil as needed. Sprinkle with sugar to serve.

COOK'S TIPS
* Use leftover bread for this tasty breakfast or brunch dish.

* For a savoury version, use white bread and omit the spice and sugar; serve with tomato ketchup, or with bacon and maple syrup.

Breakfast Bruschetta

Preparation Time 5 minutes • Cooking Time 5 minutes • Serves 4 • Per Serving 145 calories, 1g fat (of which 0g saturates), 30g carbohydrate, 0.4g salt • Vegetarian • Easy

1 ripe banana, peeled and sliced
250g (9oz) blueberries
200g (7oz) quark cheese
**4 slices pumpernickel or wheat-
   free wholegrain bread**
1 tbsp runny honey

1. Put the banana into a bowl with the blueberries. Spoon in the quark cheese and mix well.

2. Toast the slices of bread on both sides, then spread with the blueberry mixture. Drizzle with the honey and serve immediately.

Banana & Pecan Muffins

Preparation Time 10 minutes • Cooking Time 20 minutes • Makes 12 muffins • Per Muffin 236 calories, 9g fat (of which 4g saturates), 37g carbohydrate, 0.8g salt • Vegetarian • Easy

275g (10oz) self-raising flour
1 tbsp bicarbonate of soda
1 tsp salt
3 very ripe large bananas, about 450g (1lb), peeled and mashed
125g (4oz) golden caster sugar
1 large egg
50ml (2fl oz) milk
75g (3oz) melted butter
50g (2oz) chopped roasted pecan nuts

1. Preheat the oven to 180°C (160°C fan oven) mark 4. Line a muffin tin with 12 paper cases. Sift together the flour, bicarbonate of soda and salt and set aside.

2. Combine the bananas, sugar, egg and milk, then pour in the melted butter and mix well. Add to the flour mixture with the nuts, stirring quickly and gently with just a few strokes. Half-fill the muffin cases.

3. Bake for 20 minutes or until golden and risen. Transfer to a wire rack and leave to cool

COOK'S TIP
The secret to really light, fluffy muffins is a light hand:
• Be sure to sift the flour.
• Stir the mixture as little as possible; it's okay if it looks a little lumpy.
• Over-mixing will give tough, chewy results.

Brazil Nut & Banana Smoothie

Preparation Time 10 minutes • Serves 2, makes 600ml (1 pint) • Per Serving 310 calories, 19g fat (of which 4g saturates), 25g carbohydrate, 0.3g salt • Vegetarian • Easy

6 shelled Brazil nuts
1 lemon
1 small ripe banana
1 small ripe avocado
1 tsp clear honey
400ml (14fl oz) low-fat dairy or soya milk, well chilled
2 tsp wheatgerm

1. Grind the nuts in a spice grinder or food processor – the mixture needs to be very fine to obtain a good blend.

2. Using a sharp knife, cut off the peel from the lemon, removing as much of the white pith as possible. Chop the flesh roughly, discarding any pips. Peel and roughly chop the banana. Halve the avocado and remove the stone. Peel and roughly chop.

3. Put the nuts, lemon, banana and avocado into a blender with the honey and milk. Whiz until smooth. Pour into two glasses and sprinkle with the wheatgerm.

COOK'S TIP
This is a lusciously thick, protein-rich drink; add more milk if you like.

Berry Uplifter

Preparation Time 5 minutes • Serves 1, makes 400ml (14fl oz) • Per Serving 277 calories,
2g fat (of which trace saturates), 62g carbohydrate, 0.1g salt • Vegetarian • Easy

**175g (6oz) blueberries, thawed if
frozen, juices reserved (see
Cook's Tip, page 9)**
**50g (2oz) cranberries, thawed if
frozen, juices reserved**
**200ml (7fl oz) freshly pressed
orange juice or 2 medium
oranges, juiced**
1 tbsp wheatgerm
1–2 tsp thick honey

1. If using fresh berries, wash and
pat them dry with kitchen paper
and put into a blender. If the fruit
has been frozen, add the juices
as well.

2. Pour in the orange juice and
add 2 tsp wheatgerm. Whiz
until smooth.

3. Taste and add honey to
sweeten. Pour into a glass and
serve sprinkled with the remaining
wheatgerm.

**TRY SOMETHING
DIFFERENT**
*Use blackberries instead of
blueberries: they are also an
excellent source of vitamin C.*

Cranberry & Mango Smoothie

Preparation Time 5 minutes • Serves 2 • Per Serving 133 calories, 1g fat (of which trace saturates), 29g carbohydrate, 0.2g salt • Vegetarian • Easy

1 ripe mango, peeled, stoned and chopped
250ml (9fl oz) cranberry juice
150g (5oz) natural yogurt

1. Put the mango into a blender with the cranberry juice and whiz for 1 minute.

2. Add the yogurt and whiz until smooth, then serve.

COOK'S TIP

If you're on a dairy-free diet or are looking for an alternative to milk-based products, swap the yogurt for soya yogurt. Soya is a good source of omega-3 and omega-6 essential fatty acids, and can help to lower cholesterol levels.

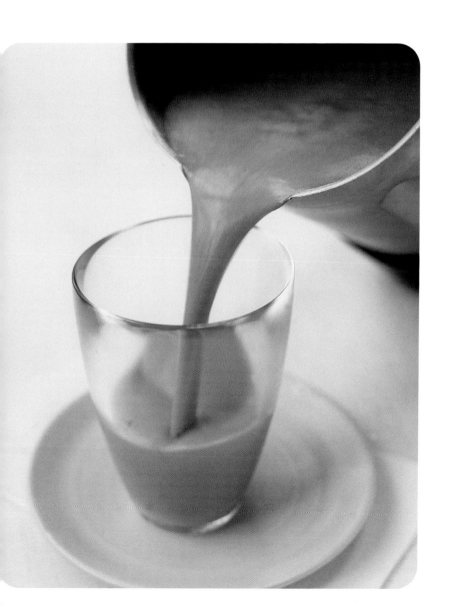

Green Tea Pick-me-up

Preparation Time 10 minutes, plus infusing and cooling • Serves 1, makes 300ml (½ pint) • Per Serving 99 calories, trace fat, 24g carbohydrate, 0g salt • Vegetarian • Easy

1 tsp, or 1 teabag, Japanese green tea
1 ripe kiwi fruit
8 fresh lychees
a few ice cubes

1. Put the tea or teabag into a heatproof jug and pour in 200ml (7fl oz) boiling water. Leave to infuse for 3 minutes, then strain to remove the tea leaves, or discard the teabag. Leave to cool.

2. When ready to serve, peel and roughly chop the kiwi fruit. Put into a blender. Peel the lychees, then cut in half and remove the stones.

3. Add to the blender with the cold tea. Whiz until smooth, then pour over ice in a glass to serve.

TRY SOMETHING DIFFERENT
For extra zing, add a 5cm (2in) piece fresh root ginger, peeled and chopped, to the blender in step 2.

Mango & Oat Smoothie

Preparation Time 5 minutes • Serves 2 • Per Serving 145 calories, 2g fat (of which 1g saturates), 27g carbohydrate, 0.2g salt • Vegetarian • Easy

150g (5oz) natural yogurt
1 small mango, peeled, stoned and chopped
2 tbsp oats
4 ice cubes

1. Put the yogurt into a blender. Set aside a little chopped mango to decorate, if you like, and add the remaining mango, oats and ice cubes to the yogurt. Whiz until smooth. Serve immediately, decorated with chopped mango.

TRY SOMETHING DIFFERENT
Instead of mango, use 2 nectarines or peaches, or 175g (6oz) soft seasonal fruits such as raspberries, strawberries or blueberries.

Mega Vitamin C Tonic

Preparation Time 10 minutes • Serves 1, makes 200ml (7fl oz) • Per Serving 144 calories, trace fat, 35g carbohydrate, 0g salt • Vegetarian • Easy

1 large orange
1 lemon
1 lime
½ pink grapefruit
1–2 tsp clear honey
crushed ice
slices of citrus fruit to decorate

1. Using a sharp knife, cut off the peel from all the citrus fruit, removing as much of the white pith as possible. Chop the flesh roughly, discarding any pips, and put into a blender.

2. Add the honey to taste and whiz for a few seconds until smooth.

3. Pour over crushed ice in a glass and decorate with citrus fruit to serve.

TRY SOMETHING DIFFERENT
For a refreshing, longer and less concentrated drink, divide this smoothie between two glasses and top up with sparkling mineral water.

Morning-after Detoxer

Preparation Time 10 minutes • Serves 2, makes 600ml (1 pint) • Per Serving 115 calories,
1g fat (of which trace saturates), 26g carbohydrate, 0.2g salt • Vegetarian • Easy

**200g (7oz) cooked, peeled baby
beetroot in natural juice**
**15g (½oz) fresh root ginger, peeled
and roughly chopped**
juice of 1 lemon
**150ml (¼ pint) freshly pressed
carrot juice or 2 medium carrots,
250g (9oz), juiced**
**150ml (¼ pint) freshly pressed
apple juice or 2 dessert apples,
juiced**

1. Roughly chop the beetroot and
put into a blender with the juices
from the pack.

2. Add the ginger, pour in the
carrot and apple juices and whiz
until smooth. Pour into two glasses
and serve immediately.

COOK'S TIP
*If you find the drink is too
concentrated, thin it with a little
chilled water.*

**TRY SOMETHING
DIFFERENT**
*For a more powerful detoxer, juice
225g (8oz) raw beetroot and a
5cm (2in) piece of peeled fresh root
ginger and mix with the other juices.*

BRUNCH & LUNCH

Apple, Celery, Ham & Pecan Salad

Preparation Time 10 minutes • Serves 6 • Per Serving 340 calories, 28g fat (of which 3g saturates), 10g carbohydrate, 1.6g salt • Easy

450g (1lb) fennel, halved
2 large Braeburn or Cox's Orange Pippin apples, about 450g (1lb), quartered, cored and sliced
75g (3oz) shelled pecan nuts
300g (11oz) cooked ham, cut into wide strips
1 head chicory, divided into leaves
fresh flat-leafed parsley sprigs to garnish

FOR THE POPPY SEED DRESSING
1 tsp clear honey
2 tsp German or Dijon mustard
3 tbsp cider vinegar
9 tbsp vegetable oil
2 tsp poppy seeds
salt and ground black pepper

1. To make the dressing, whisk together the honey, mustard, vinegar and seasoning in a small bowl. Whisk in the oil, then the poppy seeds. Set to one side.

2. Remove the central core from the fennel and slice thinly, lengthways. Place the fennel, apples, nuts, ham and chicory in a large serving bowl. Toss with the dressing and adjust the seasoning if necessary. Garnish with parsley sprigs and serve immediately.

TRY SOMETHING DIFFERENT
• For a meat-free alternative, replace the ham with 150g (5oz) cubed Gruyère or Cheddar cheese.
• *Spicy Cumin Dressing*
Mix 3 tbsp red wine vinegar with 1 tsp ground cumin, a pinch of caster sugar and 5 tbsp olive oil. Season with salt and pepper to taste.
• *Balsamic Dressing*
Mix 3 tbsp balsamic vinegar with 2 tbsp olive oil and 2 tsp wholegrain mustard.

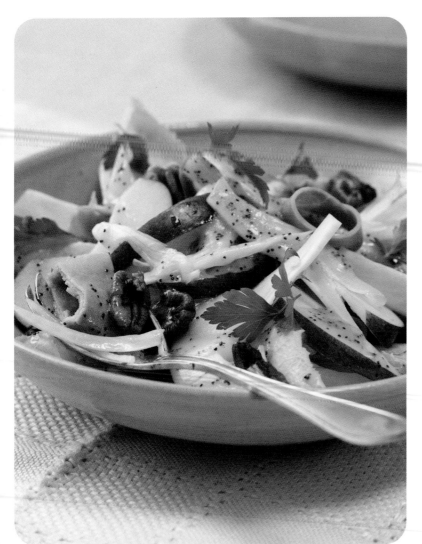

Chickpea & Beetroot Salad

Preparation Time 15 minutes • Serves 4 • Per Serving 266 calories, 12g fat (of which 3g saturates), 32g carbohydrate, 0.7g salt • Vegetarian • Easy

250g (9oz) cooked and peeled beetroot in natural juice, roughly chopped
400g can chickpeas, drained and rinsed
50g (2oz) sultanas
20g (¾oz) fresh basil
1 medium carrot, grated

½ small white cabbage, finely shredded
juice of ½ lemon
150g (5oz) Greek yogurt
20g (¾oz) fresh mint, finely chopped
2 tbsp extra virgin olive oil
salt and ground black pepper

1. Put the beetroot and chickpeas into a large bowl. Add the sultanas, tear the basil and add, then add the carrot, cabbage and lemon juice.

2. Put the yogurt into a separate bowl. Add the mint and oil and season with salt and pepper. Spoon on to the salad and mix everything together. Serve immediately.

TRY SOMETHING DIFFERENT
• *Use parsley instead of basil, and add 4 finely chopped spring onions.*
• *Scatter the salad with 2 tbsp lightly toasted pumpkin seeds or sunflower seeds.*

Bacon & Egg Salad

Preparation Time 10 minutes • Cooking Time 10 minutes • Serves 4 • Per Serving 360 calories,
27g fat (of which 8g saturates), 9g carbohydrate, 3.1g salt • Easy

4 medium eggs
250g (9oz) rindless smoked bacon
150g (5oz) cherry tomatoes
2 slices thick-cut sourdough bread,
**   with crusts removed**
2 tbsp mayonnaise
juice of ½ lemon
25g (1oz) Parmesan, freshly grated
2 Little Gem lettuces
ground black pepper

1. Heat a pan of water until simmering, add the eggs and boil for 6 minutes. Cool completely under cold water, peel and set aside.

2. Meanwhile, heat a griddle pan, then fry the bacon for 5 minutes or until crisp. Remove from the pan, chop into large pieces and leave to cool.

3. Add the tomatoes and bread to the pan and fry for 2–3 minutes until the bread is crisp and the tomatoes are starting to char. Remove from the heat, chop the bread into bite-sized croûtons and set aside.

4. To make the dressing, put the mayonnaise into a bowl and squeeze in the lemon juice. Add the Parmesan and mix, then season with pepper.

5. Separate the lettuce leaves and put into a large bowl. Add the bacon, tomatoes and croûtons, toss lightly, then divide among four plates. Cut the eggs in half and add one egg to each plate. Drizzle the dressing over the salad and serve.

Bacon, Avocado & Pinenut Salad

Preparation Time 5 minutes • Cooking Time 7 minutes • Serves 4 • Per Serving 352 calories,
34g fat (of which 6g saturates), 3g carbohydrate, 1g salt • Easy

**125g (4oz) streaky bacon rashers,
   rind removed, cut into small neat
   pieces (lardons)**
1 shallot, finely chopped
120g bag mixed baby salad leaves
1 ripe avocado
50g (2oz) pinenuts
4 tbsp olive oil
4 tbsp red wine vinegar
salt and ground black pepper

1. Put the bacon lardons into a frying pan over a medium heat for 1–2 minutes until the fat starts to run. Add the shallot and fry gently for about 5 minutes or until golden.

2. Meanwhile, divide the salad leaves among four plates. Halve, stone and peel the avocado, then slice the flesh. Arrange on the salad leaves.

3. Add the pinenuts, oil and vinegar to the frying pan and let bubble for 1 minute. Season with salt and pepper.

4. Tip the bacon, pinenuts and dressing over the salad and serve at once, while still warm.

**TRY SOMETHING
DIFFERENT**
Replace the pinenuts with walnuts.

Bean & Chorizo Salad

Preparation Time 15 minutes • Serves 4 • Per Serving 295 calories, 19g fat (of which 4g saturates), 20g carbohydrate, 1.9g salt • Easy

400g can borlotti beans, drained and rinsed
4 large celery sticks, finely sliced
75g (3oz) chorizo sausage, diced
2 shallots, finely chopped
2 tbsp freshly chopped flat-leafed parsley
grated zest of ½ lemon, plus 1 tbsp lemon juice
4 tbsp extra virgin olive oil
salt and ground black pepper

1. Put the borlotti beans into a large bowl and add the celery, chorizo, shallots and parsley.

2. To make the dressing, whisk together the lemon zest, lemon juice and oil in a small bowl. Season with salt and pepper and whisk again to combine.

3. Pour the dressing over the bean mixture, toss together and serve.

TRY SOMETHING DIFFERENT
Use mixed beans or flageolet beans instead of borlotti beans.

Chicken, Avocado & Peanut Salad

Preparation Time 15 minutes, plus chilling • Serves 4 • Per Serving 335 calories, 28g fat (of which 4g saturates), 2g carbohydrate, 0.1g salt • Easy

2 roast chicken breasts, about 250g (9oz) total weight, skinned and sliced
75g (3oz) watercress
2 tbsp cider vinegar
1 tsp English ready-made mustard
5 tbsp groundnut oil
1 large ripe avocado, halved, stoned, peeled and thickly sliced
50g (2oz) roasted salted peanuts, roughly chopped
salt and ground black pepper

1. Arrange the sliced chicken on top of the watercress, cover with clingfilm and chill until ready to serve.

2. Put the vinegar, mustard and oil into a bowl, season with salt and pepper and whisk together. Add the avocado and gently toss in the dressing, making sure each slice of avocado is well coated.

3. Just before serving, spoon the avocado and dressing over the chicken and watercress. Sprinkle with the chopped peanuts and serve immediately.

Spring Chicken Salad with Sweet Chilli Sauce

Preparation Time 15 minutes • Cooking Time 10 minutes • Serves 4 • Per Serving 307 calories, 15g fat (of which 3g saturates), 8g carbohydrate, 0.2g salt • Easy

2 tbsp groundnut oil, plus extra to grease
4 boneless, skinless chicken breasts, each cut into four strips
1 tbsp Cajun seasoning (see Cook's Tips)
salt and ground black pepper

FOR THE SALAD
175g (6oz) small young carrots, cut into thin matchsticks
125g (4oz) cucumber, halved lengthways, seeded and cut into matchsticks
6 spring onions, cut into matchsticks
10 radishes, sliced
50g (2oz) bean sprouts, rinsed and dried
50g (2oz) unsalted peanuts, roughly chopped
1 large red chilli, finely chopped (see Cook's Tips)
2 tsp sesame oil
Thai chilli dipping sauce to drizzle

1. Soak eight bamboo skewers in water for 20 minutes. Oil a baking sheet.

2. Preheat the grill. Toss the chicken strips in the Cajun seasoning, then season with salt and pepper and brush with oil. Thread on to the skewers.

3. Place the skewered chicken strips on the prepared baking sheet and cook under the hot grill for 3–4 minutes on each side until cooked through.

4. Place all the salad vegetables, peanuts and red chilli in a bowl, toss with the sesame oil and season well with salt and pepper.

5. Divide the vegetables among four plates, top with the warm chicken skewers and drizzle with the chilli sauce. Serve immediately.

COOK'S TIPS
• *Cajun seasoning is a spice and herb mixture including chilli, cumin, cayenne and oregano.*
• *Chillies vary enormously in strength, from quite mild to blisteringly hot, depending on the type of chilli and its ripeness. Taste a small piece first to check it's not too hot for you.*
• *Be extremely careful when handling chillies not to touch or rub your eyes with your fingers, or they will sting. Wash knives immediately after handling chillies. As a precaution, use rubber gloves when preparing them, if you like.*

Easy Chicken Salad

Preparation Time 10 minutes • Serves 1 • Per Serving 323 calories, 18g fat (of which 5g saturates), 17g carbohydrate, 0.9g salt • Easy

100g (3½oz) shredded roast chicken, skin discarded
1 carrot, chopped
1 celery stick, chopped
¼ cucumber, chopped
a handful of ripe cherry tomatoes, chopped
1 tbsp hummus
¼ lemon to serve

1. Put the chicken into a shallow bowl. Add the carrot, celery, cucumber and cherry tomatoes.

2. Top with the hummus and serve with lemon for squeezing over the salad.

TRY SOMETHING DIFFERENT
• *For an even more nutritious salad, add a few pumpkin seeds or sunflower seeds, or a handful of sprouted seeds such as alfalfa, or chopped watercress.*
• *For extra bite, add a little finely chopped red chilli; for extra sweetness, add some strips of red pepper.*
• *For extra flavour, add some chopped coriander or torn basil leaves.*

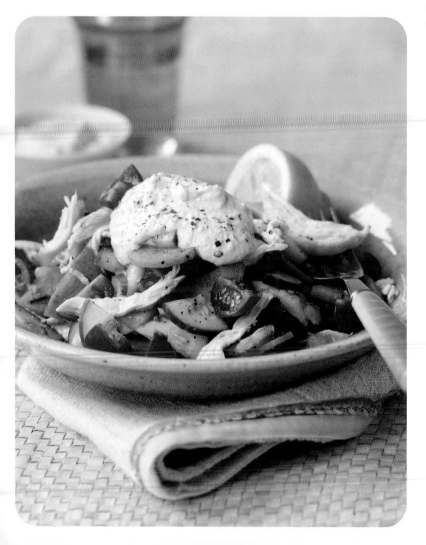

Spring Lamb & Flageolet Bean Salad

Preparation Time 5 minutes • Cooking Time 10–20 minutes, plus resting • Serves 4 • Per Serving 535 calories, 35g fat (of which 11g saturates), 17g carbohydrate, 1.4g salt • Easy

2–3 lamb fillets, about 700g (1½lb) in total
1 tbsp Dijon mustard
5 tbsp olive oil
1 tsp freshly chopped parsley
2 garlic cloves
juice of 1 lemon
400g can flageolet or cannellini beans, drained and rinsed
125g (4oz) frisée lettuce or curly endive
250g (9oz) baby plum or cherry tomatoes, halved
salt and ground black pepper

1. Rub the lamb fillets with the mustard and season with pepper. Put 1 tbsp oil in a non-stick frying pan and fry the lamb over a medium heat for 5–7 minutes on each side for medium-rare, 8–10 minutes for well done. Remove the lamb, cover and set aside for 5 minutes. This allows the meat to relax, which makes slicing easier.

2. To make the dressing, put the parsley, garlic, lemon juice and remaining oil into a food processor and whiz for 10 seconds. Alternatively, put the ingredients into a screw-topped jar, screw on the lid and shake to combine.

3. Put the beans, frisée or curly endive and the tomatoes into a bowl, combine with the dressing and season to taste with salt and pepper.

4. Slice the lamb into 1cm (½in) pieces and place on top of the flageolet salad. Serve immediately.

TRY SOMETHING DIFFERENT
For a vegetarian alternative, skewer the whole tomatoes on soaked wooden kebab sticks, alternating with small balls of mozzarella cheese. Grill the kebabs and drizzle with 2 tbsp pesto sauce thinned with a little olive oil.

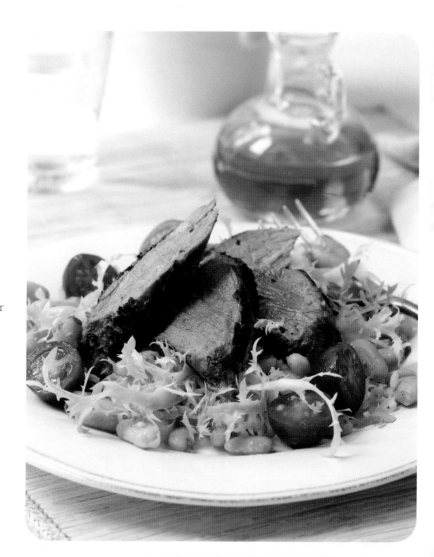

Chilli Beef Noodle Salad

Preparation Time 15 minutes, plus soaking • Serves 4 • Per Serving 286 calories, 11g fat (of which 2g saturates), 33g carbohydrate, 0.8g salt • Easy

150g (5oz) dried rice noodles
juice of 1 lime
1 lemongrass stalk, outside leaves
   discarded, finely chopped
1 red chilli, seeded and chopped
   (see Cook's Tips, page 38)
2 tsp finely chopped fresh root
   ginger
2 garlic cloves, crushed
1 tbsp Thai fish sauce
3 tbsp extra virgin olive oil
50g (2oz) rocket
125g (4oz) sliced cold roast beef
125g (4oz) sunblush tomatoes,
   chopped
salt and ground black pepper

1. Put the noodles into a large bowl. Pour boiling water over them to cover, then put to one side for 15 minutes.

2. Meanwhile, in a small bowl, whisk together the lime juice, lemongrass, chilli, ginger, garlic, fish sauce and oil. Season with salt and pepper.

3. While they are still warm, drain the noodles well, put into a large bowl and toss with the dressing. Allow to cool.

4. Just before serving, toss the rocket, sliced beef and chopped tomatoes with the noodles.

COOK'S TIP
Sunblush tomatoes are partly dried, and more moist than sun-dried tomatoes.

Oriental Beef Salad

Preparation Time 10 minutes • Cooking Time 10 minutes • Serves 4 • Per Serving 214 calories, 9g fat (of which 3g saturates), 9g carbohydrate, 2.8g salt • Easy

4 tbsp tamari (wheat-free Japanese soy sauce), plus extra to serve
juice of ½ lime
2 sirloin steaks, about 175g (6oz) each
1 tbsp vegetable oil
1 mango, peeled, stoned and sliced
4 spring onions, sliced
½ Chinese lettuce, finely sliced
150g (5oz) bean sprouts
1 tbsp sesame seeds, toasted
2 tbsp freshly chopped coriander
lime wedges to serve

1. Put the tamari and lime juice into a bowl and mix well. Spoon half the dressing over the steaks and set the remainder aside.

2. Heat the oil in a frying pan, add the steaks and fry for 3 minutes on each side for medium-rare, or 3–4 minutes for well done. Set aside.

3. Put the mango, spring onions, lettuce and bean sprouts into a large bowl. Add the remaining dressing and toss gently.

4. Slice the steak into 1cm (½in) strips and serve with the salad. Sprinkle with sesame seeds and coriander and serve with a wedge of lime. Serve extra tamari sauce in a small bowl.

TRY SOMETHING DIFFERENT
For an alternative dressing, mix 2 tbsp tamari with 1 tbsp clear honey and 1 tbsp mirin (sweet Japanese rice wine).

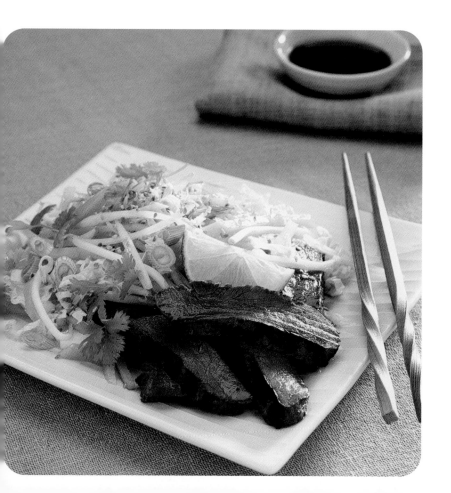

Guacamole Salad

Preparation Time 15 minutes • Cooking Time 20 minutes • Serves 6 • Per Serving 317 calories,
28g fat (of which 9g saturates), 7g carbohydrate, 1.3g salt • Easy

**3 beef tomatoes, each sliced
  horizontally into six**
½ small onion, finely sliced
1 garlic clove, crushed
**1 tbsp fresh coriander leaves, plus
  extra sprigs to garnish**
4 ripe avocados
juice of 1 lime
200g (7oz) feta cheese, crumbled
**100g (3½oz) sunblush tomatoes
  in oil**
salt and ground black pepper
lime wedges to serve

1. Divide the tomato slices among six serving plates, then scatter the onion, garlic and coriander leaves over them.

2. Cut each avocado into quarters as far as the stone. Keeping the avocado whole, start at the pointed end and peel away the skin. Separate each quarter, remove the stone, then slice the pieces lengthways. Squeeze the lime juice over the slices to stop them from browning and arrange on the plates.

3. Top with the feta cheese, sunblush tomatoes and a sprig of coriander. Finish each salad with a drizzle of oil reserved from the sunblush tomatoes and season well with salt and pepper. Serve with lime wedges.

Goat's Cheese & Walnut Salad

Preparation Time 10 minutes • Serves 6 • Per Serving 428 calories, 41g fat (of which 10g saturates), 3g carbohydrate, 0.5g salt • Easy

1 large radicchio, shredded
2 bunches of prepared watercress,
   about 125g (4oz) total weight
1 red onion, finely sliced
150g (5oz) walnut pieces
200g (7oz) goat's cheese, crumbled

FOR THE DRESSING
2 tbsp red wine vinegar
8 tbsp olive oil
a large pinch of caster sugar
salt and ground black pepper

1. Whisk all the ingredients for the dressing in a small bowl and put to one side.

2. Put the radicchio, watercress and onion into a large bowl. Pour the dressing over the salad and toss well.

3. To serve, divide the salad among six plates and sprinkle the walnuts and goat's cheese on top.

Parma Ham, Onion & Rocket Salad

Preparation Time 10 minutes • Serves 4 • Per Serving 237 calories, 18g fat (of which 6g saturates), 4g carbohydrate, 1.4g salt • Easy

150g (5oz) Italian marinated onions, drained, reserving 1 tbsp of the marinade (see Cook's Tips)
4 tbsp olive oil
200g (7oz) rocket
8 slices Parma ham, about 100g (3½oz)
75g (3oz) Parmesan shavings
salt and ground black pepper

1. To make the dressing, place the reserved marinade from the onions, the oil, salt and pepper into a bowl and whisk together until combined.

2. Put the onions into a large bowl with the rocket, Parma ham and dressing. Toss together and divide among four plates. Scatter the Parmesan shavings on top and serve at once.

COOK'S TIPS
• *Jars of Italian marinated onions in balsamic vinegar are available in larger supermarkets and Italian delis.*
• *Parmesan shavings can be bought in supermarkets. To make your own, use a vegetable peeler to pare off shavings from a block of Parmesan.*

Smoked Mackerel Salad

Preparation Time 15 minutes • Serves 4 • Per Serving 656 calories, 56g fat (of which 10g saturates), 16g carbohydrate, 2.4g salt • Easy

250g (9oz) cooked, peeled baby
   beetroot in natural juice, diced
1 tbsp olive oil
2 tsp white wine vinegar
350g (12oz) potato salad
1–2 tbsp lemon juice
4 peppered smoked mackerel
   fillets, skinned and flaked
2 tbsp freshly chopped chives, plus
   extra to garnish
salt and ground black pepper

1. Put the beetroot into a bowl. Sprinkle with the oil and vinegar, season with salt and pepper and toss together.

2. Mix the potato salad with the lemon juice to taste. Season with salt and pepper, add the mackerel and chives and toss together.

3. Pile the mackerel mixture into four bowls. Sprinkle the beetroot over the salad and garnish with chives.

Throw-it-all-together Chicken Salad

Preparation Time 10 minutes • Serves 4 • Per Serving 215 calories, 9g fat (of which 2g saturates), 9g carbohydrate, 0.6g salt • Easy

4 chargrilled chicken breasts, about 125g (4oz) each, torn into strips
2 carrots, cut into strips
½ cucumber, halved lengthways, seeded and cut into ribbons
a handful of fresh coriander leaves, roughly chopped
½ head of Chinese leaves, shredded

4 handfuls of watercress
4 spring onions, shredded

FOR THE DRESSING
5 tbsp peanut butter
2 tbsp sweet chilli sauce
juice of 1 lime
salt and ground black pepper

1. Put the chicken strips and all the salad ingredients into a large salad bowl.

2. To make the dressing, put the peanut butter, chilli sauce and lime juice into a small bowl and mix well. Season with salt and pepper. If the dressing is too thick to pour, add 2–3 tbsp cold water, a tablespoon at a time, to thin it – use just enough water to make the dressing the correct consistency.

3. Drizzle the dressing over the salad, toss gently together and serve.

COOK'S TIPS
• Use leftover roast chicken or beef, or cooked ham.
• Use washed and prepared salad instead of the Chinese leaves and watercress.

Tuna, Bean & Red Onion Salad

Preparation Time 5 minutes • Serves 4 • Per Serving 190 calories, 6g fat (of which 1g saturates), 15g carbohydrate, 1.1g salt • Easy

400g can cannellini beans, drained and rinsed
1 small red onion, very finely sliced
1 tbsp red wine vinegar
225g can tuna steak in oil (see Cook's Tip)
2 tbsp freshly chopped parsley
salt and ground black pepper
green salad and warm crusty bread to serve

1. Put the cannellini beans, onion and vinegar into a bowl, season with a little salt and mix well. Add the tuna with its oil, breaking the fish into large flakes.

2. Add half the parsley and season generously with pepper. Toss the salad, then scatter the remaining parsley over the top. Serve with a green salad and plenty of warm crusty bread.

COOK'S TIP
Buy tuna steak canned in extra virgin olive oil, which flakes easily into large, meaty flakes and has a good flavour.

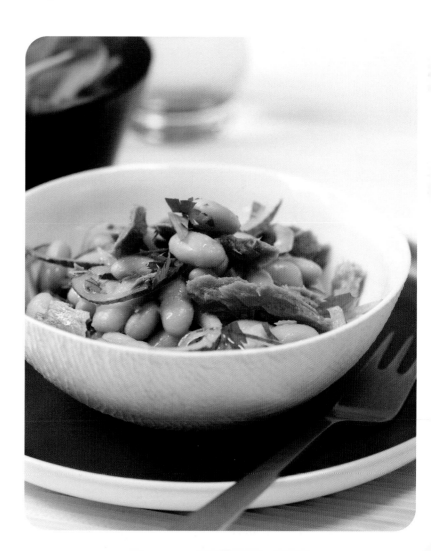

Warm Broad Bean & Feta Salad

Preparation Time 10 minutes • Cooking Time 5 minutes • Serves 2 • Per Serving 321 calories,
22g fat (of which 8g saturates), 15g carbohydrate, 1.8g salt • Vegetarian • Easy

**225g (8oz) broad beans – if using
fresh beans you will need to start
with 700g (1½lb) pods**
**100g (3½oz) vegetarian feta
cheese, chopped**
2 tbsp freshly chopped mint
2 tbsp extra virgin olive oil
a squeeze of lemon juice
salt and ground black pepper
lemon wedges to serve

1. Cook the beans in lightly salted
boiling water for 3–5 minutes
until tender. Drain, then plunge
them briefly into cold water and
drain again.

2. Tip the beans into a bowl and
add the feta, mint, oil and lemon
juice. Season well with salt and
pepper and toss together. Serve
with lemon wedges.

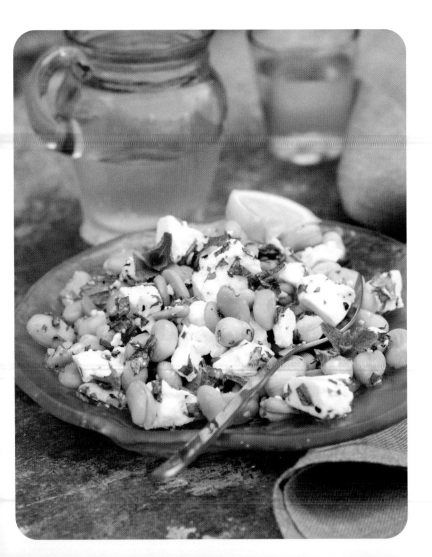

Warm Lentil Salad

Preparation Time 15 minutes • Cooking Time 10 minutes • Serves 2 • Per Serving 300 calories,
10g fat (of which 2g saturates), 33g carbohydrate, trace salt • Vegetarian • Easy

2 medium eggs
2 tsp olive oil
2 small leeks, trimmed and
   chopped
4 spring onions, chopped
1 red pepper, seeded and chopped
400g can lentils, drained
150ml (¼ pint) vegetable stock
a handful of rocket leaves
salt and ground black pepper

1. Gently lower the eggs into a pan of boiling water, then reduce the heat and simmer for 7 minutes.

2. Meanwhile, heat the oil in a separate pan and fry the leeks, spring onions and red pepper for 6–8 minutes until softened.

3. Stir in the lentils and stock and bring to the boil, then reduce the heat and simmer for 1–2 minutes. Shell the eggs, then cut in half. Season the lentil mixture with salt and pepper, then divide between two bowls and top each with an egg and a few rocket leaves.

Warm Pear & Walnut Caesar Salad

Preparation Time 10 minutes • Cooking Time 5 minutes • Serves 6 • Per Serving 397 calories,
31g fat (of which 8g fat saturates), 19g carbohydrate, 1.3g salt • Easy

50g (2oz) walnut pieces
1 tbsp walnut or mild olive oil
a small knob of butter
3 firm rosy pears, quartered, cored
    and thickly sliced
1 bag Caesar salad with croûtons,
    dressing and Parmesan
100g (3½oz) blue cheese, such as
    Roquefort, Stilton or Danish blue,
    crumbled
1 bunch of chives, roughly chopped

1. Put the walnuts into a non-stick frying pan and dry-fry over a medium heat for about 1 minute until lightly toasted. Set aside.

2. Heat the oil and butter in the frying pan, then add the pears. Fry for 2 minutes on each side or until golden. Remove with a slotted spoon.

3. To serve, put the salad leaves into a large bowl. Add the walnuts, pears, croûtons, Parmesan and blue cheese. Add the salad dressing and toss lightly, or serve the dressing separately in a small bowl. Serve immediately, garnished with chives.

GET AHEAD

To prepare ahead Complete the recipe to the end of step 2, then leave the pears in the frying pan and set aside for up to 4 hours.
To use Warm the pears in the pan for 1 minute, then complete the recipe.

Warm Bacon Salad

Preparation Time 10 minutes • Cooking Time 10–15 minutes • Serves 2 • Per Serving 375 calories,
29g fat (of which 9g saturates), 11g carbohydrate, 1.7g salt • Easy

4 handfuls of soft salad leaves
1 small red onion, thinly sliced
75g (3oz) cubed pancetta
1 thick slice white bread, diced
2 medium eggs
25g (1oz) Parmesan shavings (see
    Cook's Tips, page 46)
salt and ground black pepper

FOR THE DRESSING
1 tbsp Dijon mustard
2 tbsp red wine vinegar
2 tbsp fruity olive oil

1. Put the salad leaves and onion into a large bowl. Fry the pancetta in a non-stick frying pan until it begins to release some fat. Add the diced bread and continue to fry until the pancetta is golden and crisp.

2. Put all the dressing ingredients into a small bowl, season with salt and pepper and whisk together.

3. Half-fill a small pan with cold water and bring to the boil. Turn the heat right down – there should be just a few bubbles on the base of the pan. Break the eggs into a cup, then tip them gently into the pan and cook for 3–4 minutes, using a metal spoon to baste the tops with a little of the hot water. Lift the eggs out of the water with a slotted spoon and drain on kitchen paper.

4. Tip the pancetta, bread and any pan juices over the salad leaves. Add the Parmesan, then pour the dressing over the salad. Toss well, then divide between two plates. Top each with an egg, season to taste and serve.

Warm Spicy Chorizo & Chickpea Salad

Preparation Time 15 minutes • Cooking Time about 15 minutes • Serves 6 • Per Serving 365 calories, 24g fat (of which 6g saturates), 27g carbohydrate, 1.3g salt • Easy

5 tbsp olive oil
200g (7oz) chorizo or spicy
   sausage, thinly sliced
225g (8oz) red onion, chopped
1 large red pepper, seeded and
   roughly chopped
3 garlic cloves, finely chopped

1 tsp cumin seeds
2 × 400g cans chickpeas, drained
   and rinsed
2 tbsp freshly chopped coriander
juice of 1 lemon
salt and ground black pepper

1. Heat 1 tbsp oil in a non-stick frying pan and cook the chorizo or spicy sausage over a medium heat for 1–2 minutes until lightly browned. Remove the chorizo with a slotted spoon and put to one side. Fry the onion in the chorizo oil for 8–10 minutes until browned.

2. Add the red pepper, garlic, cumin and chickpeas to the onion and cook for a further 5 minutes, stirring frequently to prevent sticking.

3. Remove the pan from the heat and add the chorizo, coriander, lemon juice and remaining oil. Season well and serve immediately.

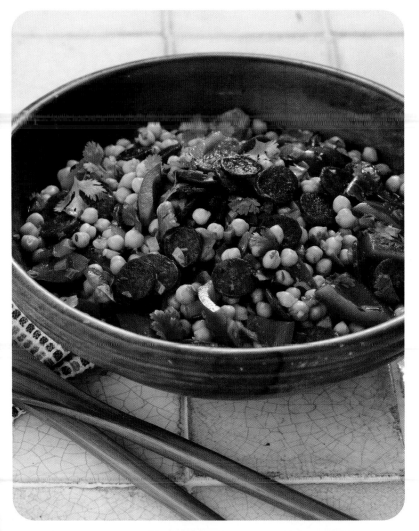

Salmon Niçoise

Preparation Time 15 minutes • Cooking Time 6 minutes • Serves 4 • Per Serving 290 calories,
16g fat (of which 3g saturates), 16g carbohydrate, 1.7g salt • Easy

4 medium eggs
400g can mixed beans, drained and rinsed
50g (2oz) pitted black olives
250g (9oz) cherry tomatoes, halved
a large handful of mixed salad leaves
1 tbsp olive oil
juice of ½ lemon
200g (7oz) cooked salmon flakes
salt and ground black pepper

1. Cook the eggs in a pan of simmering water for 6 minutes. Drain the eggs, then shell and cut into quarters.

2. Put the beans into a salad bowl with the olives, tomatoes and salad leaves. Add the oil and lemon juice, season with salt and pepper and toss together. Divide among four plates, add the egg and salmon and serve.

TRY SOMETHING DIFFERENT
For a more traditional Niçoise salad, replace the salmon with a 300g (11oz) fresh tuna steak, cooked and flaked, and use 250g (9oz) cooked green beans instead of the mixed beans. Scatter with chopped anchovy fillets and flat-leafed parsley.

Roasted Vegetable Tartlets

Preparation Time 15 minutes • Cooking Time about 7 minutes • Makes 6 • Per Tartlet 356 calories, 24g fat (of which 1g saturates), 30g carbohydrate, 1.1g salt • Vegetarian • Easy

375g pack ready-rolled puff pastry, thawed if frozen

plain flour to dust

1 medium egg, beaten

2 tbsp coarse sea salt

300g (11oz) vegetable antipasti in olive oil

olive oil, if needed

2 tbsp balsamic vinegar

190g tub red pepper hummus

50g (2oz) wild rocket

salt and ground black pepper

1. Preheat the oven to 220°C (200°C fan oven) mark 7. Unroll the puff pastry on a lightly floured surface and cut it into six squares. Put the pastry squares on a large baking sheet and prick each one all over with a fork. Brush the surface with beaten egg and sprinkle the edges with sea salt. Bake for 5–7 minutes until the pastry is golden brown and cooked through. Press down the centre of each tartlet slightly with the back of a fish slice.

2. Make the dressing. Pour 4 tbsp oil from the jar of antipasti into a bowl (top it up with a little more olive oil if there's not enough in the antipasti jar). Add the vinegar, season with salt and pepper and mix well, then set aside.

3. To serve, spread some hummus over the central part of each tartlet. Put the tartlets on individual plates and spoon on the antipasti – there's no need to be neat. Whisk the balsamic vinegar dressing. Add the rocket leaves and toss to coat, then pile a small handful of leaves on top of each tartlet. Serve immediately.

GET AHEAD

*To **prepare ahead** Complete the recipe to the end of step 1. Leave the tartlets to cool on a wire rack, then store in an airtight container. It will keep for up to two days.*
To use Complete the recipe.

Egg & Pepper Pizza

Preparation Time 15 minutes • Cooking Time 12 minutes • Serves 4 • Per Serving 403 calories,
13g fat (of which 2g saturates), 61g carbohydrate, 1g salt • Vegetarian • Easy

150g (5oz) red and yellow marinated peppers in oil, drained and oil reserved
8 tbsp passata
4 small wheat-free pizza bases
4 medium eggs
125g (4oz) watercress, washed and stalks removed

1. Preheat the oven to 220°C (200°C fan oven) mark 7. Put two large baking sheets, big enough to hold two pizzas each, into the oven to heat up.

2. Chop the peppers into thin strips. Spoon 2 tbsp passata over each pizza base and scatter strips of pepper around the edges. Make a dip in the passata in the middle of each pizza and break an egg into it. Carefully slide the pizzas on to the preheated baking sheets. Place in the oven and cook for 12 minutes or until the egg is thoroughly cooked.

3. Top the pizzas with the watercress, drizzle with a little of the reserved oil from the peppers and serve.

COOK'S TIP
Watercress is the salad superfood par excellence. It is a good source of iron, and vitamins C and E.

Eggs Benedict

Preparation Time 15 minutes • Cooking Time 10 minutes • Serves 4 • Per Serving 402 calories,
33g fat (of which 18g saturates), 14g carbohydrate, 1.6g salt • Easy

4 slices bread
4 medium eggs
150ml (¼ pint) Hollandaise Sauce
   (see Cook's Tip)
4 thin slices lean ham
parsley sprigs to garnish

1. Toast the bread on both sides. Poach the eggs. Gently warm the Hollandaise Sauce.

2. Top each slice of toast with a folded slice of ham, then with a poached egg. Finally, coat with Hollandaise Sauce.

3. Garnish each with a sprig of parsley and serve.

TRY SOMETHING DIFFERENT
Eggs Florentine
Cook 900g (2lb) washed spinach in a pan with a little salt until tender. Drain well, chop and reheat with 15g (½oz) butter. Melt 25g (1oz) butter, stir in 3 tbsp plain flour and cook gently for 1 minute, stirring. Remove from the heat and gradually stir in 300ml (½ pint) milk. Bring to the boil and cook, stirring, until thickened. Add 50g (2oz) grated Gruyère cheese or Cheddar and season. Do not allow to boil. Poach the eggs. Place the spinach in an ovenproof dish, arrange the eggs on top and pour the cheese sauce over them. Sprinkle with 25g (1oz) grated cheese and brown under the grill.

COOK'S TIP
Hollandaise Sauce
Put 4 tbsp white wine vinegar, a blade of mace, 1 slice of onion, 1 bay leaf and 6 black peppercorns into a pan. Bring to the boil and reduce to 1 tbsp liquid. Cut 150g (5oz) unsalted butter into 10 pieces. Put 3 medium egg yolks into a heatproof bowl with 1 piece of butter and a pinch of salt. Beat, then strain in the vinegar mixture. Place over a pan of hot water, making sure the base of the bowl doesn't touch the water. Whisk for 3 minutes until pale and starting to thicken. Add a piece of butter and beat until completely absorbed. Repeat with the remaining pieces of butter. Make sure the sauce doesn't get too hot during cooking. Season and add lemon juice to taste. Serves 6.

Courgette & Parmesan Frittata

Preparation Time 10 minutes • Cooking Time 15–20 minutes • Serves 4 • Per Serving 229 calories,
19g fat (of which 9g saturates), 2g carbohydrate, 0.6g salt • Vegetarian • Easy

40g (1½oz) butter
1 small onion, finely chopped
225g (8oz) courgettes, finely sliced
6 medium eggs, beaten
25g (1oz) Parmesan, freshly grated,
plus shavings to garnish (see
Cook's Tips, pages 46 and 190)
salt and ground black pepper
green salad to serve

1. Melt 25g (1oz) butter in an 18cm
(7in) non-stick frying pan and cook
the onion for about 10 minutes or
until softened. Add the courgettes
and fry gently for 5 minutes or until
they begin to soften.

2. Beat the eggs in a bowl and
season with salt and pepper.

3. Add the remaining butter to
the pan and heat, then pour in the
eggs. Cook for 2–3 minutes until
golden underneath and cooked
around the edges. Meanwhile,
preheat the grill to medium.

4. Sprinkle the grated cheese over
the frittata and grill for 1–2 minutes
until just set. Scatter with Parmesan
shavings, cut into quarters and
serve with a green salad.

**TRY SOMETHING
DIFFERENT**
Cherry Tomato and Rocket Frittata
Replace the courgettes with 175g
(6oz) ripe cherry tomatoes, frying
them for 1 minute only, until they
begin to soften. Immediately after
pouring in the eggs, scatter 25g
(1oz) rocket leaves over the surface.
Continue cooking as in step 3.

Potato & Chorizo Tortilla

Preparation Time 5 minutes • Cooking Time 25 minutes • Serves 4 • Per Serving 431 calories, 32g fat (of which 7g saturates), 23g carbohydrate, 0.9g salt • Easy

6 tbsp olive oil
450g (1lb) potatoes, very thinly
   sliced
225g (8oz) onions, thinly sliced
2 garlic cloves, finely chopped
50g (2oz) chorizo sausage, cut into
   thin strips
6 large eggs, lightly beaten
salt and ground black pepper

1. Heat the oil in an 18cm (7in) non-stick frying pan over a medium-low heat. Add the potatoes, onions and garlic and stir together until coated in the oil. Cover the pan, then cook gently, stirring from time to time, for 10–15 minutes until the potato is soft. Season with salt, then add the chorizo.

2. Preheat the grill until hot. Season the beaten eggs with salt and pepper, then pour over the potato mixture. Cook over a medium heat for 5 minutes or until the edges are beginning to brown and the egg is about three-quarters set. Put the pan under the grill to brown the top. The egg should be a little soft in the middle, as it continues to cook and set as it cools. Leave to cool.

3. Using a flexible turner or spatula, carefully loosen the tortilla around the edge and underneath. Cut into wedges and serve.

Mixed Mushroom Frittata

Preparation Time 15 minutes • Cooking Time 15–20 minutes • Serves 4 • Per Serving 148 calories, 12g fat (of which 3g saturates), 0g carbohydrate, 0.3g salt • Vegetarian • Easy

1 tbsp olive oil
300g (11oz) mixed mushrooms, sliced
2 tbsp freshly chopped thyme
zest and juice of ½ lemon
50g (2oz) watercress, chopped
6 medium eggs, beaten
salt and ground black pepper
stoneground wholegrain bread (optional) and a crisp green salad to serve

1. Heat the oil in a large deep frying pan over a medium heat. Add the mushrooms and thyme and stir-fry for 4–5 minutes until starting to soften and brown. Stir in the lemon zest and juice, then bubble for 1 minute. Lower the heat.

2. Preheat the grill. Add the watercress to the beaten eggs, season with salt and pepper and pour into the pan. Cook on the hob for 7–8 minutes until the sides and base are firm but the centre is still a little soft.

3. Transfer to the grill and cook for 4–5 minutes until just set. Cut into wedges and serve with chunks of bread, if you like, and a salad.

Thai Chicken Soup

Preparation Time 5 minutes • Cooking Time 17 minutes • Serves 4 • Per Serving 175 calories,
7g fat (of which 1g saturates), 7g carbohydrate, 1.2g salt • Easy

1 tbsp vegetable oil
1 small onion, sliced
300g (11oz) stir-fry chicken pieces
1–2 tbsp Thai red curry paste
600ml (1 pint) hot chicken stock
400g can chopped plum tomatoes
100g (3½oz) sugarsnap peas,
 halved if large
150g (5oz) baby sweetcorn, halved
 if large
4 tbsp freshly chopped coriander
grated zest of ½ lime, plus 4 lime
 wedges to serve

1. Heat the oil in a large frying pan or wok over a medium heat. Add the onion and fry for 5 minutes or until it begins to soften. Add the chicken and cook for a further 5 minutes or until golden brown, then add the curry paste and fry for another minute to warm the spices through and release the flavours.

2. Pour in the hot stock and tomatoes, then simmer for 5 minutes. Add the sugarsnap peas and sweetcorn and cook for a further minute or so until the chicken is cooked through. Divide the soup among four warmed bowls, sprinkle with the coriander and lime zest, and serve with lime wedges to squeeze over the soup.

Teriyaki Tuna with Noodle Broth

Preparation Time 10 minutes • Cooking Time 10 minutes • Serves 4 • Per Serving 411 calories,
11g fat (of which 3g saturates), 43g carbohydrate, 0.6g salt • Easy

2 tbsp teriyaki marinade

juice of ½ lime

1 tbsp sweet chilli sauce

1 tbsp honey

4 tuna steaks, 125g (4oz) each

**750ml (1¼ pints) hot vegetable
    stock**

2 tbsp dry sherry

200g (7oz) medium egg noodles

**200g (7oz) pak choi, roughly
    chopped**

2 carrots, cut into matchsticks

**250g (9oz) button mushrooms,
    sliced**

**freshly chopped coriander
    (optional)**

1. Mix the teriyaki marinade with the lime juice, chilli sauce and honey in a large shallow dish. Add the tuna and toss to coat.

2. Put the hot stock and the sherry into a pan and bring to the boil. Add the noodles and cook for 4–5 minutes, then stir in the pak choi, carrots and mushrooms and simmer for 1 minute.

3. Meanwhile, heat a frying pan until hot. Fry the tuna in the marinade for 2 minutes on each side or until just cooked and still slightly pink inside. Cut into thick slices.

4. When the noodles are cooked, divide among four wide bowls and spoon the broth over them. Top each with the tuna and a sprinkling of coriander, if you like, and serve.

Broccoli & Goat's Cheese Soup

Preparation Time 10 minutes • Cooking Time 20 minutes • Serves 6 • Per Serving 220 calories, 16g fat (of which 10g saturates), 8g carbohydrate, 0.5g salt • Easy

50g (2oz) butter
2 medium onions, chopped
1 litre (1¾ pints) vegetable, chicken or turkey stock
700g (1½lb) broccoli, broken into florets, stout stalks peeled and chopped
1 head of garlic, separated into cloves, unpeeled
1 tbsp olive oil
150g (5oz) goat's cheese
salt and ground black pepper

1. Preheat the oven to 200°C (180°C fan oven) mark 6. Melt the butter in a pan over a gentle heat. Add the onions, then cover the pan and cook for 4–5 minutes until translucent. Add half the stock and bring to the boil. Add the broccoli and return to the boil, then cover the pan, reduce the heat and simmer for 15–20 minutes until the broccoli is tender.

2. Toss the cloves of garlic in the oil and tip into a roasting tin. Roast in the oven for 15 minutes or until soft when squeezed.

3. Leave the soup to cool a little, then add the goat's cheese and whiz in batches in a blender or food processor until smooth. Return the soup to the pan and add the remaining stock. Reheat gently on the hob and season to taste with salt and pepper.

4. Ladle the soup into warmed bowls, squeeze the garlic out of their skins and scatter over the soup, add a sprinkling of black pepper and serve.

TRY SOMETHING DIFFERENT
• *Double the quantity of goat's cheese if you prefer a stronger taste.*
• *Instead of goat's cheese, substitute a soft garlic cheese for a really garlicky flavour.*

Full-of-goodness Broth

Preparation Time 10 minutes • Cooking Time 6–8 minutes • Serves 4 • Per Serving 107 calories,
4g fat (of which trace saturates), 9g carbohydrate, 1g salt • Vegetarian • Easy

1–2 tbsp medium curry paste (see
Cook's Tip)
200ml (7fl oz) reduced-fat coconut
milk
600ml (1 pint) hot vegetable stock
200g (7oz) smoked tofu, cubed
2 pak choi, chopped
a handful of sugarsnap peas
4 spring onions, chopped
lime wedges to serve

1. Heat the curry paste in a pan for
1–2 minutes. Add the coconut milk
and hot stock and bring to the boil.

2. Add the smoked tofu, pak choi,
sugarsnap peas and spring onions.
Reduce the heat and simmer for
1–2 minutes.

3. Ladle into warmed bowls and
serve with a wedge of lime to
squeeze over the broth.

**TRY SOMETHING
DIFFERENT**
*Replace the smoked tofu with
shredded leftover roast chicken
and simmer for 2–3 minutes.*

COOK'S TIP
*Check the ingredients in the curry
paste: some may not be suitable for
vegetarians.*

SNACKS & LIGHT BITES

Artichoke & Goat's Cheese Toasts

Preparation Time 15 minutes • Cooking Time 3 minutes • Serves 4 • Per Serving 371 calories,
22g fat (of which 11g saturates), 26g carbohydrate, 2.1g salt • Easy

**225g jar marinated artichoke
hearts in oil, drained (oil
reserved) and sliced (see Cook's
Tips)**
**225g (8oz) firm goat's cheese, rind
removed, diced**
**1 tbsp freshly chopped thyme
leaves, plus extra thyme sprigs
to garnish**

**grated zest of 1 lemon, plus 1 tbsp
lemon juice**
½ tsp wholegrain mustard
**4 thick slices flavoured bread, such
as olive or rosemary**
**75g (3oz) Serrano or Parma ham
slices**
salt and ground black pepper
olive oil to drizzle
crushed black pepper to garnish

1. Halve the artichokes and put
into a large bowl with the goat's
cheese and chopped thyme.

2. Whisk together the lemon zest
and juice, mustard and 3 tbsp of
the reserved artichoke oil. Season
with salt and pepper and whisk
to combine, then stir into the
artichoke mixture.

3. Toast the bread on both sides.
Divide the artichoke mixture
among the slices of toast and
arrange the ham on top. Drizzle
with a little olive oil, garnish with
thyme sprigs and crushed black
pepper and serve immediately.

COOK'S TIPS

• *Find marinated artichokes in
supermarkets; alternatively, buy
canned artichoke hearts, drain, slice
and cover in olive oil. They will keep
in the fridge for up to one week.*
• *Serrano ham is Spanish cured
ham, made in the same way as
Parma ham.*

Croque Monsieur

Preparation Time 5 minutes • Cooking Time 8 minutes • Serves 2 • Per Serving 551 calories,
35g fat (of which 22g saturates), 27g carbohydrate, 3.6g salt • Easy

4 slices white bread
butter, softened, to spread, plus
**   extra for frying**
Dijon mustard, to taste
125g (4oz) Gruyère cheese
4 slices ham

1. Spread each slice of bread on both sides with the butter. Then spread one side of two slices of bread with a little Dijon mustard.

2. Divide the cheese and ham between the two mustard-spread bread slices. Top each with the remaining bread and press down.

3. Heat a griddle with a little butter until hot and fry the sandwiches for 2–3 minutes on each side until golden and crispy and the cheese starts to melt. Slice in half and serve immediately.

Bruschetta with Tapenade

Preparation Time 10 minutes • Cooking Time 5 minutes • Makes 12 • Per Slice 119 calories, 4g fat (of which trace saturates), 19g carbohydrate, 0.7g salt • Easy

1 ciabatta loaf
olive oil to brush
6 tbsp tapenade (see Cook's Tips)
selection of vegetable antipasti,
**   such as marinated red peppers**
**   and artichokes, drained**
a few basil sprigs to garnish

1. Cut the ciabatta on the diagonal to make 12 slices. Brush both sides of the slices with a little oil. Heat a griddle pan until hot, add the ciabatta slices and toast for a couple of minutes on each side.

2. Spread a thin layer of tapenade on each slice of bread, then top with a little of the antipasti. Garnish with basil and serve. Alternatively, arrange the antipasti in separate bowls and let your guests assemble their own bruschettas.

COOK'S TIPS
• *Tapenade is a black olive paste from Provence in the south of France. You can buy ready-made tapenade, or make your own by whizzing 75g (3oz) pitted black olives in a food processor with 4 anchovies, 2 tbsp olive oil and 1 tbsp freshly chopped flat-leafed parsley.*
• *Instead of spreading it on bread, serve tapenade as a dip for crisp raw carrots, red pepper strips or chicory leaves.*

Grilled Ciabatta & Mozzarella Salad

Preparation Time 10 minutes • Cooking Time 5 minutes • Serves 4 • Per Serving 613 calories, 33g fat (of which 13g saturates), 56g carbohydrate, 2.4g salt • Vegetarian • Easy

8 thick slices Italian bread, such
   as ciabatta
2 tsp olive paste or sun-dried
   tomato paste
2 × 150g packs mozzarella cheese,
   drained and sliced (see Cook's
   Tips, page 190)
4 tbsp olive oil, plus extra to drizzle

2 tbsp balsamic vinegar
280g jar marinated artichoke
   hearts in oil, drained and sliced
   (see Cook's Tips, page 70)
100g (3½oz) rocket salad
50g (2oz) sun-dried tomato halves
salt and ground black pepper

1. Preheat the grill. Toast the bread slices on one side. Spread the untoasted side with olive or sun-dried tomato paste, then top with mozzarella slices and drizzle lightly with oil.

2. Mix the vinegar, salt and pepper in a bowl and whisk in the 4 tbsp oil. Add the artichoke hearts.

3. Place the bread slices under the grill for 2–3 minutes until the mozzarella browns lightly.

4. Toss the rocket salad with the artichoke mixture and divide among four plates. Top with two slices of grilled bread and the sun-dried tomatoes and serve.

Veggie Pitta

Preparation Time 8 minutes • Serves 1 • Per Serving 322 calories, 11g fat (of which 2g saturates), 47g carbohydrate, 1.2g salt • Vegetarian • Easy

1 wholemeal pitta bread
1 tbsp hummus (to make your own, see page 78), plus extra to serve
15g (½oz) unsalted cashew nuts
2 closed-cup mushrooms, finely sliced
¼ cucumber, chopped
fresh watercress or mixed salad leaves
ground black pepper

1. Split the pitta bread and spread with the hummus.

2. Fill the pitta with the cashew nuts, mushrooms, cucumber and a generous helping of fresh watercress or salad leaves. Serve with extra hummus, if you like, and season with pepper.

TRY SOMETHING DIFFERENT
Add a diced ripe avocado. It is rich in omega fats and good for your skin.

Tomato Crostini with Feta & Basil

Preparation Time 20 minutes • Cooking Time 3 minutes • Serves 4 • Per Serving 242 calories,
17g fat (of which 3g saturates), 18g carbohydrate, 1.5g salt • Vegetarian • Easy

1 small garlic clove, crushed
3 tbsp freshly chopped basil, plus
extra basil leaves to garnish
25g (1oz) pinenuts
2 tbsp extra virgin olive oil
grated zest and juice of 1 lime
50g (2oz) vegetarian feta cheese
4 large tomatoes, preferably vine-
ripened, thickly sliced
150g tub fresh tomato salsa
50g (2oz) pitted black olives,
roughly chopped
4 thick slices country-style bread
salt and ground black pepper

1. Put the garlic, chopped basil, pinenuts, oil, lime zest and juice into a food processor and whiz to a smooth paste. Add the feta cheese and whiz until smooth. Thin with 1 tbsp water if necessary. Season with salt and pepper.

2. Put the tomatoes, salsa and olives into a bowl and gently toss together.

3. Toast the bread. Divide the tomato mixture among the slices of toast and spoon the basil and feta mixture on top. Garnish with basil leaves and serve.

Chicken & Salsa Verde Crostini

Preparation Time 20 minutes, plus chilling • Cooking Time 2 minutes • Makes 15 • Per Serving 208 calories, 9g fat (of which 1g saturates), 24g carbohydrate, 1.7g salt • Easy

50g (2oz) walnuts

1 loaf walnut bread, cut into
    15 × 1cm (½in) slices

2 tbsp olive oil

1 tbsp sea salt flakes

175g (6oz) cooked chicken breast,
    thinly sliced

125g (4oz) sun-dried tomatoes in
    oil, drained and thinly sliced

freshly chopped flat-leafed parsley
    to garnish

FOR THE SALSA VERDE

3 tbsp each roughly chopped fresh
    coriander, mint and basil

1 garlic clove, roughly chopped

2 tbsp Dijon mustard

3 anchovy fillets

1 tbsp capers

50ml (2fl oz) olive oil

juice of ½ lemon

1. Put the walnuts into a dry pan and toast over a medium-high heat, tossing regularly, for 2–3 minutes until golden brown. Chop finely and set aside.

2. Put all the salsa verde ingredients into a food processor or blender and whiz until smooth. (Alternatively, use a pestle and mortar.) Cover and chill.

3. Preheat the grill to high. Put the bread on a baking sheet, brush with oil and sprinkle with sea salt flakes. Grill for 1 minute on each side or until lightly toasted.

4. To serve, put two or three chicken slices on each crostini base, top with a spoonful of salsa verde and slices of sun-dried tomato, then garnish with a sprinkling of walnuts and flat-leafed parsley.

Easy Wrap

Preparation Time 10 minutes • Serves 4 • Per Serving 269 calories, 16g fat (of which 3g saturates), 17g carbohydrate, 1.7g salt • Easy

1 tsp salt

1 tsp ground black pepper

2 cooked chicken breasts, about 125g (4oz) each, cut into bite-size pieces

1 carrot, grated

1 avocado, halved, stoned, peeled and chopped

a small handful of rocket

juice of ½ lemon

3 tbsp mayonnaise

4 flour tortillas

1. Mix the salt with the pepper in a large bowl. Add the chicken, carrot, avocado and rocket and mix well.

2. In a separate bowl, mix the lemon juice with the mayonnaise, then spread over the tortillas. Divide the chicken mixture among the tortillas, then roll up and serve in napkins, if you like.

Hummus with Rocket & Mint

Preparation Time 15 minutes, plus chilling • Serves 6 • Per Serving 399 calories, 30g fat (of which 5g saturates), 25g carbohydrate, 0.6g salt • Vegetarian • Easy

3 tbsp sherry vinegar
75ml (2½fl oz) extra virgin olive oil
150g (5oz) wild rocket
12 small fresh mint leaves
12 Peppadew peppers (mild)
    (see Cook's Tips)
6 tbsp sliced jalapeño chillies
    (see Cook's Tips)
sesame seed flatbreads and lemon
    wedges to serve

FOR THE HUMMUS
400g can chickpeas, drained and
    rinsed
juice of 1 lemon
4 tbsp tahini (see Cook's Tips)
1 garlic clove, crushed
75ml (2½fl oz) extra virgin olive oil
salt and ground black pepper

1. To make the hummus, put the chickpeas, lemon juice, tahini, garlic and oil into a food processor. Season well with salt and pepper, then whiz to a paste. Spoon the hummus into a non-metallic bowl, then cover and chill overnight.

2. To make the salad dressing, mix the vinegar with a pinch of salt in a small bowl, then add the oil and whisk to combine. Chill overnight.

3. To serve, divide the hummus among six 150ml (¼ pint) pots. Put on to six plates. Put the rocket and mint leaves into a bowl, then drizzle the dressing over them. Divide the salad, peppers, jalapeño chillies and flatbreads among the six plates. Serve with lemon wedges.

COOK'S TIPS
• *'Peppadew' is the brand name of preserved sweet and spicy red peppers from South Africa; they are available as mild or hot, and are sold in jars.*
• *Jalapeño chillies are from Mexico; they range from hot to fiery hot and when ripe they can be dark green or red; they are usually sold in jars.*
• *Tahini is a paste made from finely ground sesame seeds. It is sold in jars.*

Pork Pittas with Salsa

Preparation Time 10 minutes • Cooking Time 10 minutes • Serves 4 • Per Serving 518 calories,
17g fat (of which 5g saturates), 58g carbohydrate, 1.3g salt • Easy

1 tbsp olive oil
500g (1lb 2oz) diced pork
4 tbsp spicy seasoning such as
   fajita seasoning
4 large pittas
100g (3½oz) Greek yogurt

FOR THE SALSA
1 ripe avocado
1 red onion, chopped
4 large tomatoes, roughly chopped
a small handful of roughly chopped
   fresh coriander
juice of 1 lime
salt and ground black pepper

1. Heat the oil in a pan over a medium heat and cook the pork, stirring, for 3–4 minutes. Add the spicy seasoning and stir to coat the pork, then cook for a further 4–5 minutes until cooked through.

2. Meanwhile, make the salsa. Halve, stone and peel the avocado, then chop. Put the onion into a bowl and add the avocado, tomatoes, coriander and lime juice. Mix well, season with salt and pepper and put to one side.

3. Toast the pittas until lightly golden, then slit down the side and stuff with the pork, a spoonful of salsa and a dollop of Greek yogurt. Serve immediately.

COOK'S TIP
Make your own spicy seasoning by mixing 1 crushed garlic clove, 1 tsp ground ginger and ½–1 tsp cayenne pepper. Toss with the pork and complete the recipe.

Roast Mushrooms with Pesto

Preparation Time 5 minutes • Cooking Time 15 minutes • Serves 4 • Per Serving 258 calories,
23g fat (of which 6g saturates), 1g carbohydrate, 0.5g salt • Easy

8 portabella mushrooms
8 tbsp fresh Pesto (see Cook's Tip)
toasted ciabatta, salad and basil
**   leaves to serve**

1. Preheat the oven to 200°C
(180°C fan oven) mark 6. Put the
mushrooms into an ovenproof dish,
then spoon 1 tbsp fresh pesto on
top of each one.

2. Pour 150ml (¼ pint) boiling
water into the dish, then cook for
15 minutes or until the mushrooms
are soft and the topping is hot.
Serve with toasted ciabatta and
salad, and scatter a few small basil
leaves over the mushrooms.

COOK'S TIP
Pesto
Put a 20g pack of roughly chopped
basil into a food processor. Add
25g (1oz) finely grated Parmesan,
50g (2oz) pinenuts and 4 tbsp extra
virgin olive oil and whiz to a rough
paste. Alternatively, grind in a pestle
and mortar. Season with salt and
plenty of ground black pepper.

Mozzarella Mushrooms

Preparation Time 2–3 minutes • Cooking Time 15–20 minutes • Serves 4 • Per Serving 137 calories, 9g fat (of which 5g saturates), 5g carbohydrate, 0.4g salt • Vegetarian • Easy

8 large portabella mushrooms
8 slices marinated red pepper
8 fresh basil leaves
150g (5oz) mozzarella cheese, cut into eight slices (see Cook's Tips, page 190)
4 English muffins, halved
salt and ground black pepper
green salad to serve

1. Preheat the oven to 200°C (180°C fan oven) mark 6. Lay the mushrooms side by side in a roasting tin and season with salt and pepper. Top each mushroom with a slice of red pepper and a basil leaf. Lay a slice of mozzarella on top of each mushroom and season again. Roast in the oven for 15–20 minutes until the mushrooms are tender and the cheese has melted.

2. Meanwhile, toast the muffin halves until golden. Put a mozzarella mushroom on top of each muffin half. Serve immediately with a green salad.

Cheesy Tuna Melt

Preparation Time 5 minutes • Cooking Time 5 minutes • Serves 1 • Per Serving 747 calories, 36g fat (of which 18g saturates), 51g carbohydrate, 3.4g salt • Easy

2 slices cholla bread

100g can tuna in sunflower oil, drained

75g (3oz) Gruyère cheese, sliced

1 tomato, sliced

salt and ground black pepper

1. Preheat the grill to high. Put the bread on a baking sheet and toast one side.

2. Turn the bread so that it is untoasted side up, then divide the tuna between the two pieces and top with the cheese and tomato.

3. Grill until the cheese is bubbling and golden. Season with salt and pepper and serve immediately.

COOK'S TIP
You can use any type of bread for this recipe.

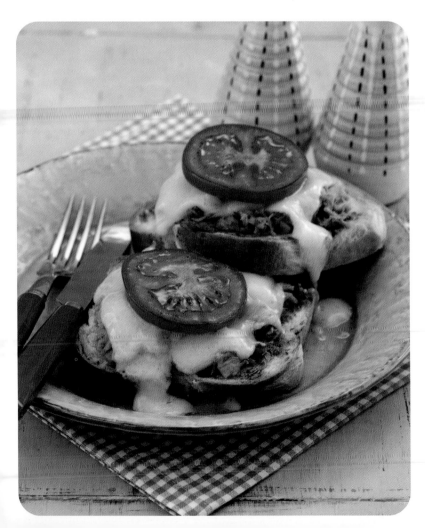

Sardines on Toast

Preparation Time 5 minutes • Cooking Time 8–10 minutes • Serves 4 • Per Serving 240 calories, 9g fat (of which 2g saturates), 25g carbohydrate, 1.6g salt • Easy

4 thick slices wholemeal bread
2 large tomatoes, sliced
2 × 120g cans sardines in olive oil,
   drained
juice of ½ lemon
a small handful of parsley, chopped

1. Preheat the grill. Toast the slices of bread on both sides.

2. Divide the tomato slices and the sardines among the toast slices, squeeze the lemon juice over them, then put back under the grill for 2–3 minutes to heat through. Scatter the parsley over the sardines and serve immediately.

TRY SOMETHING DIFFERENT
Instead of sardines, use a 200g can salmon in oil.

COOK'S TIP
Oily fish such as sardines are one of the best sources of essential heart-protecting omega-3 oils. Eat them at least once a week. Fresh Cornish sardines, when they are available, are a treat and are cheap. Look out for them at your fishmonger's or on the fresh fish counter at the supermarket.

Squid with Haricot Beans & Rocket

Preparation Time 20 minutes, plus marinating • Cooking Time about 2 minutes • Serves 6 • Per Serving 317 calories, 12g fat (of which 2g saturates), 33g carbohydrate, 1.7g salt • Easy

450g (1lb) prepared squid, cut into thick rings
3 tbsp extra virgin olive oil
1 rosemary sprig, cut into four pieces
1 chilli, seeded and finely chopped (see Cook's Tips, page 38)
zest and juice of 1 lemon

2 × 400g cans haricot beans, drained and rinsed
2 tbsp olive oil
6 slices sourdough bread
55g pack rocket
salt and ground black pepper
lemon wedges to serve

1. Put the squid into a non-metallic bowl. Add 1 tbsp extra virgin olive oil, the rosemary, chilli and half the lemon zest. Season to taste with salt and pepper, then marinate for 30 minutes.

2. Put the beans into a large bowl with the remaining lemon zest and extra virgin olive oil and the lemon juice. Season with salt and pepper, then use a potato masher to pound into a rough purée.

3. Heat the olive oil in a wok or a non-stick frying pan and cook the squid for 1–2 minutes until opaque. Toast the bread.

4. Spread the bean purée over the toast. Top with the squid and rocket and serve with lemon wedges.

Smoked Haddock Rarebit

Preparation Time 5 minutes • Cooking Time 10–15 minutes • Serves 4 • Per Serving 481 calories,
32g fat (of which 21g saturates), 16g carbohydrate, 3.4g salt • Easy

**4 × 150g (5oz) smoked haddock
   fillets, skinned**
4 slices bread
200g (7oz) spinach
2 large tomatoes, sliced
300g (11oz) low-fat crème fraîche
salt and ground black pepper

1. Preheat the grill. Season the haddock fillets with salt and pepper and put into a shallow ovenproof dish. Grill for 6–8 minutes until opaque and cooked through.

2. Toast the bread on both sides until golden.

3. Wash the spinach, squeeze out the water and put into a pan. Cover and cook for 1–2 minutes until starting to wilt. Tip into a bowl.

4. Top each piece of toast with a piece of fish, then add the tomato slices and spinach. Spoon the crème fraîche over it and grill for 2–3 minutes to heat through. Season with pepper and serve immediately.

SIMPLE SUPPERS

Fast Macaroni Cheese

Preparation Time 5 minutes • Cooking Time 15 minutes • Serves 4 • Per Serving 1137 calories, 69g fat (of which 44g saturates), 96g carbohydrate, 2g salt • Easy

500g (1lb 2oz) macaroni
500ml (18fl oz) crème fraîche
200g (7oz) freshly grated Parmesan
2 tbsp ready-made English or Dijon mustard
5 tbsp freshly chopped flat-leafed parsley
ground black pepper
green salad to serve

1. Cook the macaroni in a large pan of lightly salted boiling water according to the pack instructions. Drain and keep to one side.

2. Preheat the grill to high. Put the crème fraîche into a pan and heat gently. Stir in 175g (6oz) Parmesan, the mustard and parsley and season well with black pepper. Stir the pasta into the sauce, spoon into bowls and sprinkle with the remaining cheese. Grill until golden and serve immediately with salad.

Ham & Mushroom Pasta

Preparation Time 5 minutes • Cooking Time 15 minutes • Serves 4 • Per Serving 415 calories,
10g fat (of which 4g saturates), 67g carbohydrate, 1g salt • Easy

350g (12oz) penne pasta
1 tbsp olive oil
2 shallots, sliced
200g (7oz) small button mushrooms
3 tbsp crème fraîche
**125g (4oz) smoked ham, roughly
  chopped**
**2 tbsp freshly chopped flat-leafed
  parsley**
salt and ground black pepper

1. Cook the pasta in a large pan of lightly salted boiling water according to the pack instructions until al dente.

2. Meanwhile, heat the oil in a pan. Add the shallots and fry gently for 3 minutes or until starting to soften. Add the mushrooms and fry for 5–6 minutes.

3. Drain the pasta, put back into the pan and add the shallots and mushrooms. Stir in the crème fraîche, ham and parsley. Toss everything together, season to taste with salt and pepper and heat through to serve.

Pasta with Pesto & Beans

Preparation Time 5 minutes • Cooking Time 15 minutes • Serves 4 • Per Serving 738 calories,
38g fat (of which 10g saturates), 74g carbohydrate, 1g salt • Easy

350g (12oz) pasta shapes
175g (6oz) fine green beans,
   roughly chopped
175g (6oz) small salad potatoes,
   such as Anya, thickly sliced
250g (9oz) fresh Pesto sauce
   (see Cook's Tip, page 80)
Parmesan shavings to serve
   (see Cook's Tips, page 46)

1. Cook the pasta in a large pan of lightly salted boiling water according to the pack instructions for 5 minutes.

2. Add the beans and potatoes to the pan and continue to boil for a further 7–8 minutes until the potatoes are just tender.

3. Drain the pasta, beans and potatoes in a colander, then tip everything back into the pan and stir in the pesto sauce. Serve scattered with Parmesan shavings.

COOK'S TIP

Use leftover cooked pasta, beans or potatoes: tip the pasta into a pan of boiling water and bring back to the boil for 30 seconds. Bring the beans or potatoes to room temperature, but there's no need to re-boil them.

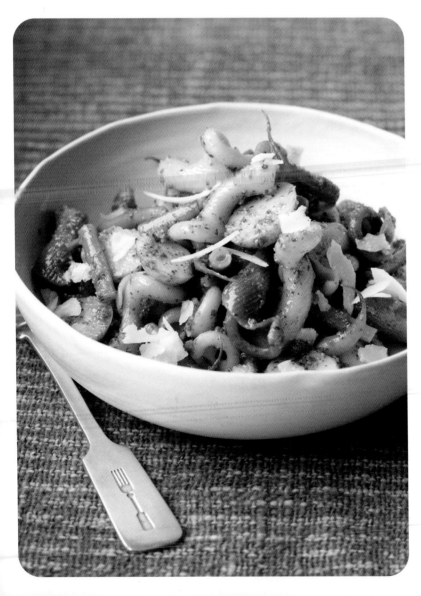

Quick & Easy Carbonara

Preparation Time 5 minutes • Cooking Time 10 minutes • Serves 4 • Per Serving 688 calories,
39g fat (of which 19g saturates), 65g carbohydrate, 1.6g salt • Easy

350g (12oz) tagliatelle
150g (5oz) smoked bacon, chopped
1 tbsp olive oil
2 large egg yolks
150ml (¼ pint) double cream
50g (2oz) freshly grated Parmesan
2 tbsp freshly chopped parsley

1. Cook the pasta in a large pan of lightly salted boiling water according to the pack instructions. Drain.

2. Meanwhile, fry the bacon in the oil for 4–5 minutes. Add to the drained pasta and keep hot.

3. Put the egg yolks into a bowl, add the cream and whisk together. Add to the pasta with the Parmesan and parsley, toss well and serve.

Creamy Parma Ham & Artichoke Tagliatelle

Preparation Time 5 minutes • Cooking Time 12 minutes • Serves 4 • Per Serving 972 calories, 56g fat (of which 36g saturates), 97g carbohydrate, 1.1g salt • Easy

500g (1lb 2oz) tagliatelle
500ml (18fl oz) crème fraîche
280g jar roasted artichoke hearts,
   drained and each cut in half
80g pack Parma ham (6 slices),
   torn into strips
2 tbsp freshly chopped sage leaves,
   plus extra to garnish
salt and ground black pepper
40g (1½oz) Parmesan shavings to
   serve (see Cook's Tips, page 46)

1. Cook the pasta in a large pan of lightly salted boiling water according to the pack instructions.

2. Drain the pasta well, leaving a ladleful of the cooking water in the pan, then put the pasta back into the pan.

3. Add the crème fraîche to the pan with the artichoke hearts, Parma ham and sage, then stir everything together. Season well.

4. Spoon the pasta into warmed bowls, sprinkle with the Parmesan shavings and garnish with sage. Serve immediately.

Pasta with Kale, Anchovy & Crispy Bread

Preparation Time 5 minutes • Cooking Time 15 minutes • Serves 4 • Per Serving 481 calories, 14g fat (of which 2g saturates), 72g carbohydrate, 3g salt • Easy

75g (3oz) fresh breadcrumbs
300g (11oz) orecchiette or other shaped pasta
150g (5oz) kale, shredded
2 tbsp olive oil
1 red chilli, seeded and finely chopped (see Cook's Tip, page 38)
100g jar anchovies, drained and chopped
25g (1oz) freshly grated Parmesan

1. Preheat the grill to medium and toast the breadcrumbs.

2. Cook the pasta in a large pan of lightly salted boiling water according to the pack instructions until al dente. Add the kale for the last 5–6 minutes of cooking time.

3. Heat 1 tbsp oil in a pan and fry the chilli and anchovies for 3–4 minutes.

4. Drain the pasta and kale, then tip back into the pan. Add the breadcrumbs, the anchovy mixture, the remaining oil and the Parmesan. Toss to mix, then serve.

Chicken, Bacon & Leek Pasta Bake

Preparation Time 10 minutes • Cooking Time about 20 minutes • Serves 4 • Per Serving 650 calories,
24g fat (of which 6g saturates), 68g carbohydrate, 2.2g salt • Easy

1 tbsp olive oil

100g (3½oz) bacon lardons

450g (1lb) boneless, skinless
chicken thighs, chopped

3 medium leeks, trimmed and
chopped

300g (11oz) macaroni or other pasta
shapes

350g carton ready-made cheese
sauce

2 tsp Dijon mustard

2 tbsp freshly chopped flat-leafed
parsley

25g (1oz) freshly grated Parmesan

1. Heat the oil in a large frying
pan. Add the bacon and chicken
and cook for 7–8 minutes. Add the
leeks and continue cooking for
4–5 minutes.

2. Meanwhile, cook the pasta in a
large pan of lightly salted boiling
water according to the pack
instructions. Drain well.

3. Preheat the grill. Add the
cheese sauce to the pasta with
the mustard, chicken mixture and
parsley. Mix well, then tip into a
2.1 litre (3¾ pint) ovenproof dish
and sprinkle with Parmesan. Grill
for 4–5 minutes until golden.

Grilled Chicken with Mango Salsa

Preparation Time 10 minutes • Cooking Time 20 minutes • Serves 4 • Per Serving 288 calories,
14g fat (of which 4g saturates), 7g carbohydrate, 0.2g salt • Easy

4 chicken breasts
juice of ½ lime
oil-water spray (see Cook's Tip)
salt and ground black pepper
rocket leaves to serve

FOR THE SALSA
1 mango, peeled, stoned and diced
1 small fennel bulb, trimmed and
   diced
1 fresh chilli, seeded and finely
   diced (see Cook's Tips, page 38)
1 tbsp balsamic vinegar
juice of ½ lime
2 tbsp freshly chopped flat-leafed
   parsley
2 tbsp freshly chopped mint

1. Put the chicken on a grill pan and season generously with salt and pepper. Sprinkle with the lime juice and spray with the oil-water blend. Grill for 8–10 minutes on each side until cooked through and the juices run clear when pierced with a skewer. Set aside.

2. Combine all the salsa ingredients in a bowl and season generously with salt and pepper. Spoon alongside the chicken and serve with rocket leaves.

COOK'S TIP

Oil-water spray is far lower in calories than oil alone and, as it sprays on thinly and evenly, you'll use less. Fill one-eighth of a travel-sized spray bottle with oil such as sunflower, light olive or vegetable (rapeseed), then top up with water. To use, shake well before spraying. Store in the fridge.

Chicken Rarebit

Preparation Time 5 minutes • Cooking Time 25 minutes • Serves 4 • Per Serving 446 calories,
24g fat (of which 14g saturates), 9g carbohydrate, 1.3g salt • Easy

**4 large chicken breasts, with skin,
about 150g (5oz) each**
15g (½oz) butter
1 tbsp plain flour
75ml (2½fl oz) full-fat milk
175g (6oz) Gruyère cheese, grated
25g (1oz) fresh white breadcrumbs
1 tsp ready-made English mustard
2 fat garlic cloves, crushed
1 medium egg yolk
**boiled new potatoes and green
beans to serve**

1. Preheat the oven to 200°C
(180°C fan oven) mark 6. Put the
chicken in a single layer into
an ovenproof dish and roast for
20 minutes or until cooked through.

2. Meanwhile, melt the butter in a
pan over a low heat, then add the
flour and stir for 1 minute. Gradually
add the milk and stir to make a
smooth sauce.

3. Add the cheese, breadcrumbs,
mustard and garlic to the sauce
and cook for 1 minute. Cool briefly,
then beat in the egg yolk. Preheat
the grill to medium-high.

4. Discard the skin from the
cooked chicken and beat any
juices from the dish into the
cheese mixture. Spread the paste
evenly over each chicken breast,
then grill for 2–3 minutes until
golden. Serve with boiled new
potatoes and green beans.

Peas & Bacon with Pan-fried Chicken

Preparation Time 5 minutes • Cooking Time 20 minutes • Serves 4 • Per Serving 314 calories, 21g fat (of which 5g saturates), 7g carbohydrate, 0.9g salt • Easy

4 skinless chicken breasts, about 125g (4oz) each
2 tbsp olive oil
2 shallots, finely sliced
3 unsmoked, rindless streaky bacon rashers, chopped
200g (7oz) frozen peas, thawed
2 tbsp sunblush tomato pesto
salt and ground black pepper
buttered new potatoes to serve

1. Heat a griddle. Season the chicken generously with salt and pepper, then brush with 1 tbsp oil and cook on the griddle, skin side down, for 8–10 minutes. Turn over and continue to cook on the other side for 8–10 minutes until cooked through and the juices run clear when the chicken is pierced with a sharp knife.

2. Meanwhile, heat the remaining oil in a frying pan and fry the shallots and bacon until the shallots are softened and the bacon is golden. Add the peas and cook for 2 minutes, then stir in the pesto.

3. Serve the peas and bacon with the chicken breasts and new potatoes.

One-pan Chicken with Tomatoes

Preparation Time 5 minutes • Cooking Time 20–25 minutes • Serves 4 • Per Serving 238 calories, 4g fat (of which 1g saturates), 20g carbohydrate, 1g salt • Easy

4 chicken thighs

1 red onion, sliced

400g can chopped tomatoes with herbs

400g can mixed beans, drained and rinsed

2 tsp balsamic vinegar

freshly chopped flat-leafed parsley to garnish

1. Heat a non-stick pan and fry the chicken thighs, skin side down, until golden. Turn over and fry for 5 minutes.

2. Add the onion and fry for 5 minutes. Add the tomatoes, mixed beans and vinegar, cover the pan and simmer for 10–12 minutes until piping hot. Garnish with parsley and serve immediately.

TRY SOMETHING DIFFERENT
Use flageolet beans or other canned beans instead of mixed beans, and garnish with fresh basil or oregano.

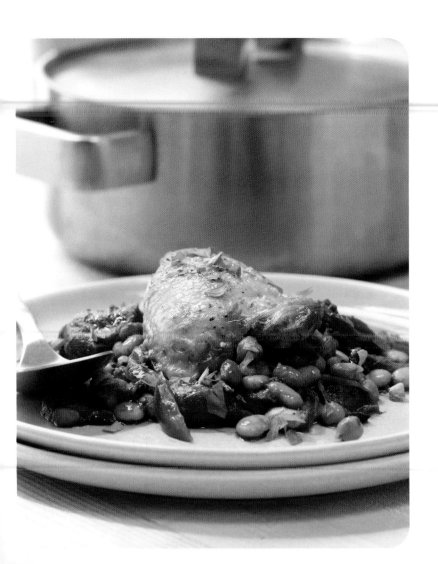

Lime & Chilli Chicken Goujons

Preparation Time 15 minutes • Cooking Time 20 minutes • Serves 4 • Per Serving 339 calories, 22g fat (of which 4g saturates), 22g carbohydrate, 1.9g salt • Easy

300g (11oz) boneless, skinless
   chicken thighs
50g (2oz) fresh breadcrumbs
50g (2oz) plain flour
2 tsp dried chilli flakes
grated zest of 1 lime
1 medium egg, beaten
2 tbsp sunflower oil
salt and ground black pepper
lime wedges to serve

FOR THE DIP
6 tbsp natural yogurt
6 tbsp mayonnaise
¼ cucumber, halved lengthways,
   seeded and finely diced
25g (1oz) freshly chopped
   coriander
 juice of 1 lime

1. Put all the dip ingredients into a bowl. Season to taste with salt and pepper and mix well, then chill.

2. Cut the chicken into strips. Put the breadcrumbs into a bowl with the flour, chilli flakes, lime zest and 1 tsp salt and mix well. Pour the egg on to a plate. Dip the chicken in egg, then coat in the breadcrumbs.

3. Heat the oil in a frying pan over a medium heat. Fry the chicken in batches for 7–10 minutes until golden and cooked through. Keep each batch warm while cooking the remainder. Transfer to a serving plate, sprinkle with a little salt, then serve with the dip and lime wedges.

COOK'S TIP

For a lower-fat version, bake the goujons in the oven. Preheat the oven to 200°C (180°C fan oven) mark 6. Put the goujons on a lightly oiled baking sheet, brush each with a little oil and bake for 12–15 minutes until golden and cooked through.

Chilli Bean Cake

Preparation Time 10 minutes • Cooking Time 20 minutes • Serves 4 • Per Serving 265 calories,
6g fat (of which 1g saturates), 41g carbohydrate, 2.1g salt • Vegetarian • Easy

3 tbsp olive oil
75g (3oz) wholemeal breadcrumbs
**1 bunch of spring onions, finely
  chopped**
**1 orange pepper, seeded and
  chopped**
**1 small green chilli, seeded and
  finely chopped (see Cook's Tips,
  page 38)**
1 garlic clove, crushed
1 tsp ground turmeric (optional)

**400g can mixed beans, drained
  and rinsed**
3 tbsp mayonnaise
**a small handful of fresh basil,
  chopped**
salt and ground black pepper

TO SERVE
soured cream
freshly chopped coriander
lime wedges (optional)

1. Heat 2 tbsp oil in a non-stick frying pan over a medium heat and fry the breadcrumbs until golden and beginning to crisp. Remove and put to one side.

2. Add the remaining oil to the pan and fry the spring onions until soft and golden. Add the orange pepper, chilli, garlic and turmeric, if using. Cook, stirring, for 5 minutes.

3. Tip in the beans, mayonnaise, two-thirds of the fried breadcrumbs and the basil. Season with salt and pepper, mash roughly with a fork, then press the mixture down to flatten and sprinkle with the remaining breadcrumbs. Fry the bean cake over a medium heat for 4–5 minutes until the base is golden. Remove from the heat, cut into wedges and serve with soured cream, coriander and the lime wedges, if you like.

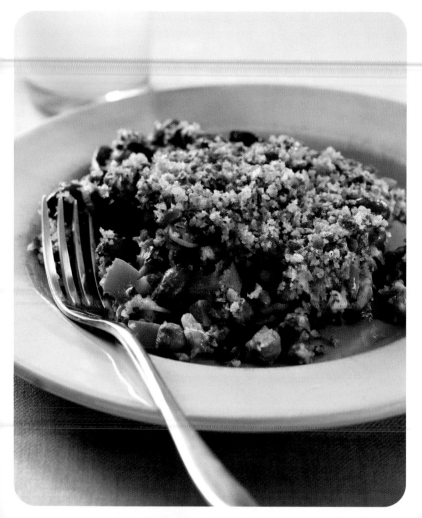

Chilli Steak & Corn on the Cob

Preparation Time 5 minutes • Cooking Time 15 minutes • Serves 4 • Per Serving 564 calories,
31g fat (of which 14g saturates), 33g carbohydrate, 1.4g salt • Easy

50g (2oz) butter, softened
1 large red chilli, seeded and
　finely chopped (see Cook's Tips,
　page 38)
1 garlic clove, crushed
25g (1oz) freshly grated Parmesan
1 tbsp finely chopped fresh basil
4 corn on the cob, each cut into
　three pieces
1 tbsp olive oil
4 sirloin steaks, about 150g (5oz)
　each
mixed green salad to serve

1. Put the butter into a bowl and beat with a wooden spoon. Add the chilli, garlic, Parmesan and basil and mix everything together. Cover and chill to firm up.

2. Meanwhile, bring a large pan of water to the boil. Add the corn, cover to bring back to the boil, then reduce the heat and simmer, half-covered, for about 10 minutes or until tender. Drain well.

3. Heat the oil in a large frying pan or griddle over a medium heat. Cook the steaks for 2–3 minutes on each side for medium-rare, or 3–4 minutes for medium.

4. Divide the corn and steaks among four warmed plates and top with the chilled butter. Serve immediately, with a mixed green salad.

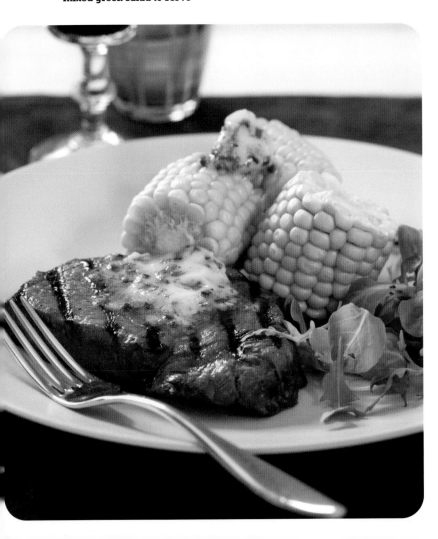

Speedy Burgers

Preparation Time 10 minutes • Cooking Time 8–12 minutes • Serves 4 • Per Serving 80 calories, 20g fat (of which 8g saturates), 2g carbohydrate, 0.3g salt • Easy

450g (1lb) lean minced beef
1 onion, very finely chopped
1 tbsp dried Herbes de Provence
2 tsp sun-dried tomato paste
1 medium egg, beaten
ground black pepper
Chilli Coleslaw to serve (see
  Cook's Tip)

1. Put the minced beef, onion, herbs, tomato paste and beaten egg into a bowl and mix well. Season with pepper, then shape the mixture into four round burgers about 2cm (¾in) thick.

2. Preheat the grill or griddle pan. Cook the burgers for 4–6 minutes on each side and serve with Chilli Coleslaw.

COOK'S TIP

Chilli Coleslaw

Put 3 peeled and finely shredded carrots into a large bowl. Add ½ finely shredded white cabbage, 1 seeded and finely sliced red pepper and ½ chopped cucumber. Mix ½ tsp harissa paste with 100g (3½oz) natural yogurt and 1 tbsp white wine vinegar. Add to the vegetables and toss well.

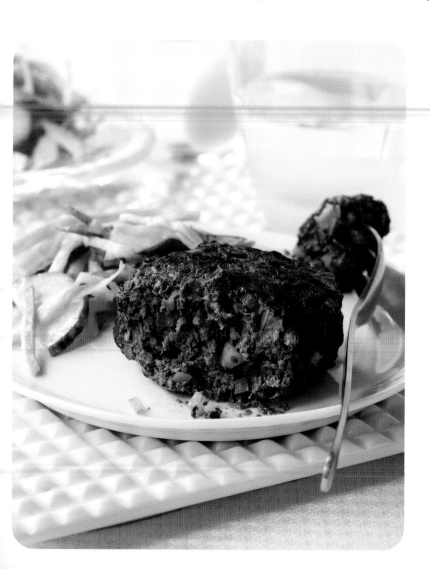

Deli Pizza

Preparation Time 5 minutes • Cooking Time 15 minutes • Serves 4 • Per Serving 440 calories,
15g fat (of which 5g saturates), 64g carbohydrate, 2.8g salt • Vegetarian • Easy

6 tbsp tomato pizza sauce
2 pizzeria-style pizza bases
100g (3½oz) soft goat's cheese
1 red onion, finely sliced
100g (3½oz) sunblush tomatoes
100g (3½oz) pitted black olives
a handful of fresh basil, roughly torn
green salad to serve

1. Preheat the oven to 220°C (200°C fan oven) mark 7. Put a large baking sheet on the top shelf to heat up.

2. Spread a thin layer of the tomato sauce over each of the pizza bases, leaving a 2.5cm (1in) border around the edge. Top with dollops of goat's cheese, then scatter the red onion, tomatoes and olives over it.

3. Slide one of the pizzas on to the hot baking sheet and bake for 15 minutes or until golden and crisp. Repeat with the second pizza base. Scatter the torn basil over each pizza and serve immediately with a green salad.

TRY SOMETHING DIFFERENT
Try marinated peppers, artichokes or chargrilled aubergines instead of the olives and sunblush tomatoes.

Mozzarella, Parma Ham & Rocket Pizza

Preparation Time 10 minutes • Cooking Time 15–18 minutes • Serves 4 • Per Serving 508 calories, 19g fat (of which 11g saturates), 64g carbohydrate, 1.9g salt • Easy

a little plain flour to dust
290g pack pizza base mix
350g (12oz) fresh tomato and chilli pasta sauce
250g (9oz) buffalo mozzarella cheese, drained and roughly chopped
6 slices Parma ham, torn into strips
50g (2oz) rocket
a little extra virgin olive oil to drizzle
salt and ground black pepper

1. Preheat the oven to 200°C (180°C fan oven) mark 6. Lightly flour two large baking sheets. Mix up the pizza base according to the pack instructions. Divide the dough into two and knead each ball on a lightly floured surface for about 5 minutes, then roll them out to make two 23cm (9in) rounds. Put each on to a prepared baking sheet.

2. Divide the tomato sauce between the pizza bases and spread it over them, leaving a small border around the edge. Scatter on the mozzarella pieces, then scatter with ham. Season well with salt and pepper.

3. Cook the pizzas for 15–18 minutes until golden. Slide on to a wooden board, top with rocket leaves and drizzle with oil. Cut in half to serve.

COOK'S TIP
If you're short of time, buy two ready-made pizza bases.

Lamb with Butter Beans & Spinach

Preparation Time 5 minutes • Cooking Time 12–15 minutes • Serves 4 • Per Serving 489 calories, 25g fat (of which 8g saturates), 29g carbohydrate, 2.1g salt • Easy

2 tbsp olive oil, plus extra to brush
1 onion, finely sliced
1 garlic clove, crushed
2 × 400g cans butter beans, drained and rinsed
200g (7oz) fresh spinach
4 small lamb chops
½ lemon, cut into wedges to serve

FOR THE DRESSING
3 tbsp low-fat natural yogurt
2 tbsp tahini (see Cook's Tips, page 78)
1 tsp harissa paste
juice of ½ lemon
salt and ground black pepper

1. Heat 1 tbsp oil in a large pan. Add the onion and fry over a medium heat for 10 minutes or until soft and golden. Add the garlic and cook for 1 minute, then add the butter beans and spinach and cook for 1–2 minutes to warm through and wilt the spinach.

2. Meanwhile, brush the lamb chops with a little oil and fry in a separate pan for 3–4 minutes on each side.

3. To make the dressing, put the remaining oil into a bowl and add the yogurt, tahini, harissa, lemon juice and 2 tbsp cold water. Season well and mix together.

4. To serve, divide the butter bean mixture among four warmed plates. Top each with a lamb chop, add a dollop of dressing and serve with the lemon wedges.

TRY SOMETHING DIFFERENT
Use cannellini or flageolet beans instead of butter beans.

Lamb Chops with Crispy Garlic Potatoes

Preparation Time 10 minutes • Cooking Time 20 minutes • Serves 4 • Per Serving 835 calories, 45g fat (of which 19g saturates), 22g carbohydrate, 0.7g salt • Easy

2 tbsp Mint Sauce (see Cook's Tips)
8 small lamb chops
3 medium potatoes, cut into 5mm (¼in) slices
2 tbsp Garlic-infused Olive Oil (see Cook's Tips)
1 tbsp olive oil
salt and ground black pepper
steamed green beans to serve

1. Spread the mint sauce over the lamb chops and leave to marinate while you prepare the potatoes.

2. Boil the potatoes in a pan of lightly salted water for 2 minutes or until just starting to soften. Drain, tip back into the pan and season with salt and pepper, then add the garlic oil and toss to combine.

3. Meanwhile, heat the olive oil in a large frying pan and fry the chops for 4–5 minutes on each side until just cooked, adding a splash of boiling water to the pan to make a sauce. Remove the chops and sauce from the pan and keep warm.

4. Add the potatoes to the pan. Fry over a medium heat for 10–12 minutes until crisp and golden. Divide the potatoes, chops and sauce among four warmed plates and serve with green beans.

COOK'S TIPS
Mint Sauce
Finely chop 20g (¾oz) fresh mint and mix with 1 tbsp each olive oil and white wine vinegar.
Garlic-infused Olive Oil
Gently heat 2 tbsp olive oil with peeled sliced garlic for 5 minutes and use immediately. Do not store.

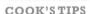

Flash-in-the-pan Pork

Preparation Time 5 minutes • Cooking Time 15 minutes • Serves 4 • Per Serving 346 calories,
12g fat (of which 4g saturates), 32g carbohydrate, 0.6g salt • Easy

700g (1½lb) new potatoes,
   scrubbed, halved if large
175g (6oz) runner beans, sliced
4 pork escalopes, about 150g (5oz)
   each
1 tbsp sunflower or olive oil
150ml (¼ pint) hot chicken stock

150ml (¼ pint) apple cider
2 tbsp wholegrain mustard
150g (5oz) Greek yogurt
4 fresh tarragon stems, leaves only
a squeeze of lemon juice
salt and ground black pepper

1. Cook the potatoes in a large pan of lightly salted boiling water for 10 minutes. Add the beans and cook for a further 5 minutes or until tender. Drain.

2. Meanwhile, season the escalopes with salt and pepper. Heat the oil in a large non-stick frying pan over a medium heat. Cook the pork for 3 minutes on each side or until browned. Remove from the pan and keep warm. Add the hot stock, cider and mustard to the pan and increase the heat to reduce the liquid by half.

3. Just before serving, reduce the heat and add the yogurt, tarragon leaves and lemon juice. Put the pork back into the pan to coat with the sauce and warm through. Serve with the potatoes and beans.

Quick Steak Supper

Preparation Time 10 minutes • Cooking Time 10 minutes • Serves 4 • Per Serving 452 calories,
17g fat (of which 6g saturates), 44g carbohydrate, 1.6g salt • Easy

2 sirloin steaks
3 tsp olive oil
4 large mushrooms, sliced
1 red onion, sliced
1 tbsp Dijon mustard
25g (1oz) butter
2 ciabattas, halved lengthways,
    then quartered, to make eight
    pieces
salt and ground black pepper
green salad to serve

1. Heat a griddle or large frying pan until very hot. Rub the steaks with 1 tsp oil, season with salt and pepper and fry for about 2 minutes on each side for rare, or 4 minutes each side for medium. Remove from the pan and leave to rest.

2. Heat the remaining oil in the pan. Add the mushrooms and red onion and fry, stirring, for 5 minutes or until softened. Stir in the Dijon mustard and butter and take off the heat.

3. Toast the ciabatta pieces on both sides. Thinly slice the steaks and divide among four pieces of ciabatta. Top with the mushrooms, onion and remaining ciabatta and serve with a green salad.

TRY SOMETHING DIFFERENT
Instead of ciabatta, serve the steak with tagliatelle or other pasta.

Speedy Beef Noodles

Preparation Time 5 minutes • Cooking Time 10 minutes • Serves 4 • Per Serving 510 calories,
19g fat (of which 5g saturates), 60g carbohydrate, 2.8g salt • Easy

250g (9oz) fine egg noodles
4 tbsp sesame oil, plus a little extra
to brush
300g (11oz) beef fillet
4 tbsp chilli soy sauce
juice of 1 lime
2 red peppers, halved, seeded and
cut into thin strips
200g (7oz) mangetouts, sliced
4 tbsp freshly chopped coriander

1. Put the noodles into a large bowl and cover with boiling water. Leave to soak for 4 minutes, then rinse under cold running water and set aside.

2. Meanwhile, brush a large frying pan or griddle with a little oil and heat until hot. Fry the beef for 3–4 minutes on each side, or 4–5 minutes if you like it well done. Remove the meat from the pan and keep warm.

3. Add the 4 tbsp oil to the pan with the chilli soy sauce, lime juice, red peppers, mangetouts and coriander and stir to mix. Add the noodles and use two large spoons to toss them over the heat to combine with the sauce and warm through.

4. Cut the beef into thin slices and serve on a bed of noodles.

Pork Stir-fry with Chilli & Mango

Preparation Time 5 minutes • Cooking Time about 10 minutes • Serves 4 • Per Serving 138 calories,
4g fat (of which 1g saturates), 17g carbohydrate, 0.8g salt • Easy

75g (3oz) medium egg noodles
1 tsp groundnut oil
½ red chilli, seeded and finely
 chopped (see Cook's Tips, here
 and on page 38)
125g (4oz) pork stir-fry strips
1 head pak choi, roughly chopped
1 tbsp soy sauce
½ ripe mango, peeled, stoned and
 sliced

1. Cook the noodles in boiling water according to the pack instructions. Drain, then plunge them into cold water and put to one side.

2. Meanwhile, heat the oil in a wok or large frying pan until very hot. Add the chilli and pork and stir-fry for 3–4 minutes. Add the pak choi and soy sauce and cook for a further 2–3 minutes. Add the mango and toss to combine.

3. Drain the noodles and add them to the pan. Toss well and cook for 1–2 minutes until heated through. Serve immediately.

COOK'S TIP
The smaller the chilli, the hotter it is.

Turkey & Sesame Stir-fry with Noodles

Preparation Time 5 minutes, plus marinating • Cooking Time 10 minutes • Serves 4 • Per Serving 672 calories, 18g fat (of which 4g saturates), 97g carbohydrate, 0.7g salt • Easy

300g (11oz) turkey breast fillets, cut into thin strips
3 tbsp teriyaki marinade
3 tbsp clear honey
500g (1lb 2oz) medium egg noodles
about 1 tbsp sesame oil, plus extra for the noodles
300g (11oz) ready-prepared mixed stir-fry vegetables, such as carrots, broccoli, red cabbage, mangetouts, bean sprouts and purple spring onions
2 tbsp sesame seeds, lightly toasted in a dry wok or heavy-based pan

1. Put the turkey strips into a large bowl with the teriyaki marinade and honey and stir to coat. Cover and set aside for 5 minutes.

2. Cook the noodles in boiling water for about 4 minutes or according to the pack instructions. Drain well, then toss in a little oil.

3. Heat 1 tbsp oil in a wok or large frying pan and add the turkey, reserving the marinade. Stir-fry over a very high heat for 2–3 minutes until cooked through and beginning to brown. Add a drop more oil, if needed, then add the vegetables and reserved marinade. Continue to cook over a high heat, stirring, until the vegetables have started to soften and the sauce is warmed through.

4. Scatter with the sesame seeds and serve immediately with the noodles.

Spiced Tikka Kebabs

Preparation Time 10 minutes • Cooking Time 20 minutes • Serves 4 • Per Serving 150 calories,
5g fat (of which 1g saturates), 4g carbohydrate, 0.3g salt • Easy

2 tbsp tikka paste

150g (5oz) natural yogurt

juice of ½ lime

4 spring onions, chopped

**350g (12oz) skinless chicken, cut
into bite-size pieces**

**lime wedges and Mixed Salad (see
Cook's Tip) to serve**

1. Preheat the grill. Put the tikka
paste, yogurt, lime juice and spring
onions into a large bowl. Add the
chicken and toss well. Thread
the chicken on to metal skewers.

2. Grill the chicken for 8–10
minutes on each side, turning and
basting with the paste, until cooked
through. Serve with lime wedges
to squeeze over the kebabs, and
Mixed Salad.

COOK'S TIP

Mixed Salad

*Put 75g (3oz) green salad leaves
into a large bowl. Add ¼ chopped
avocado, a handful of halved cherry
tomatoes, ½ chopped cucumber
and the juice of 1 lime. Season to
taste with salt and pepper and mix
together.*

Chicken, Bean & Spinach Curry

Preparation Time 10 minutes • Cooking Time about 20 minutes • Serves 4 • Per Serving 364 calories,
9g fat (of which 1g saturates), 41g carbohydrate, 2.9g salt • Easy

1 tbsp sunflower oil

350g (12oz) boneless, skinless
chicken breasts, cut into strips

1 garlic clove, crushed

300–350g tub or jar curry sauce

400g can aduki beans, drained
and rinsed

175g (6oz) ready-to-eat dried
apricots

150g (5oz) natural bio yogurt,
plus extra to serve

125g (4oz) baby spinach leaves

naan bread to serve

1. Heat the oil in a large pan over
a medium heat and fry the chicken
strips with the garlic until golden.
Add the curry sauce, beans and
apricots, then cover and simmer
gently for 15 minutes or until the
chicken is tender.

2. Over a low heat, stir in the yogurt,
keeping the curry hot without
boiling it, then stir in the spinach
until it just begins to wilt. Add a
spoonful of yogurt and serve with
naan bread.

**TRY SOMETHING
DIFFERENT**
*Use pork escalopes, cut into
thin strips, instead of chicken.*

Quick Chicken Stir-fry

Preparation Time 10 minutes • Cooking Time 12 minutes • Serves 4 • Per Serving 316 calories,
3g fat (of which 1g saturates), 46g carbohydrate, 0.5g salt • Easy

1 tsp groundnut oil
300g (11oz) boneless, skinless
    chicken breasts, sliced
4 spring onions, chopped
200g (7oz) medium rice noodles
100g (3½oz) mangetouts
200g (7oz) purple sprouting
    broccoli, chopped
2–3 tbsp sweet chilli sauce
freshly chopped coriander and
    lime wedges (optional) to
    garnish

1. Heat the oil in a wok or large frying pan. Add the chicken and spring onions and stir-fry over a high heat for 5–6 minutes until the chicken is golden.

2. Meanwhile, soak the rice noodles in boiling water for 4 minutes or according to the pack instructions.

3. Add the mangetouts, broccoli and chilli sauce to the chicken. Continue to stir-fry for 4 minutes.

4. Drain the noodles, then add to the pan and toss everything together. Scatter the chopped coriander over the top and serve with lime wedges to squeeze over the stir-fry, if you like.

TRY SOMETHING DIFFERENT
Other vegetables are just as good in this dish: try pak choi, button mushrooms, carrots cut into matchsticks, or baby sweetcorn.

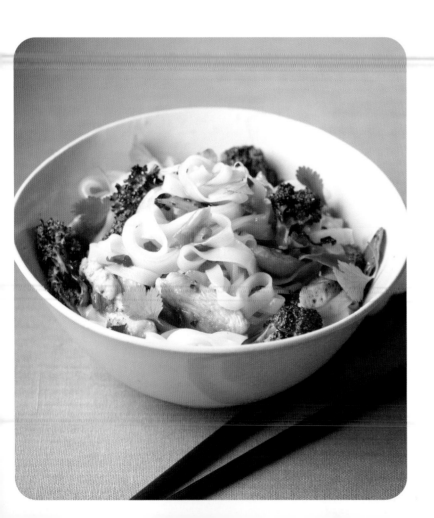

Chicken Chow Mein

Preparation Time 10 minutes • Cooking Time 10 minutes • Serves 4 • Per Serving 451 calories,
11g fat (of which 2g saturates), 59g carbohydrate, 1.3g salt • Easy

250g (9oz) medium egg noodles

1 tbsp toasted sesame oil

2 boneless, skinless chicken
    breasts, about 125g (4oz) each,
    cut into thin strips

1 bunch of spring onions, thinly
    sliced diagonally

150g (5oz) mangetouts, thickly
    sliced diagonally

125g (4oz) bean sprouts

100g (3½oz) cooked ham, finely
    shredded

120g sachet chow mein sauce

salt and ground black pepper

light soy sauce to serve

1. Cook the noodles in boiling water for 4 minutes or according to the pack instructions. Drain, rinse thoroughly in cold water, drain again and set aside.

2. Meanwhile, heat a wok or large frying pan until hot, then add the oil. Add the chicken and stir-fry over a high heat for 3–4 minutes until browned all over. Add the spring onions and mangetouts and stir-fry for 2 minutes. Stir in the bean sprouts and ham and cook for a further 2 minutes.

3. Add the drained noodles, then pour the chow mein sauce into the pan and toss together to coat evenly. Stir-fry for 2 minutes or until piping hot. Season with salt and pepper and serve immediately with light soy sauce to drizzle over the chow mein.

FISH SUPPERS

Fast Fish Soup

Preparation Time 10 minutes • Cooking Time 15 minutes • Serves 4 • Per Serving 269 calories,
10g fat (of which 2g saturates), 6g carbohydrate, 0.6g salt • Easy

1 leek, trimmed and finely sliced
4 fat garlic cloves, crushed
3 celery sticks, finely sliced
1 small fennel bulb, finely sliced
1 red chilli, seeded and finely
    chopped (see Cook's Tips,
    page 38)
3 tbsp olive oil
50ml (2fl oz) dry white wine

about 750g (1lb 10oz) mixed fish
    and shellfish, such as haddock,
    monkfish and salmon, raw
    shelled prawns, and mussels,
    scrubbed, rinsed and beards
    removed (see Cook's Tip,
    page 146)
4 medium tomatoes, chopped
1½ tbsp freshly chopped thyme
salt and ground black pepper

1. Put the leek into a large pan and add the garlic, celery, fennel, chilli and oil. Cook over a medium heat for 5 minutes or until the vegetables are soft and beginning to colour.

2. Stir in 1.1 litres (2 pints) boiling water and the wine. Bring to the boil, then reduce the heat, cover and simmer for 5 minutes.

3. Meanwhile, cut the white fish into large chunks. Add to the soup with the tomatoes and thyme. Continue to simmer gently until the fish has just turned opaque. Add the prawns and simmer for 1 minute, then add the mussels. As soon as all the mussels have opened, season the soup and ladle into warmed bowls. Discard any mussels that remain closed, then serve immediately.

COOK'S TIP
Frozen seafood mix is a useful standby. Use it instead of the fish and shellfish in this recipe but take care not to overcook or it will become tough.

TRY SOMETHING DIFFERENT
• *To give the soup more of a kick, stir in 2 tbsp Pernod instead of the wine.*
• *Garlic croûtes are traditionally served with fish soup; they can be made while the soup is simmering. Toast small slices of baguette, spread with garlic mayonnaise and sprinkle with grated cheese. Float in the hot soup just before serving.*

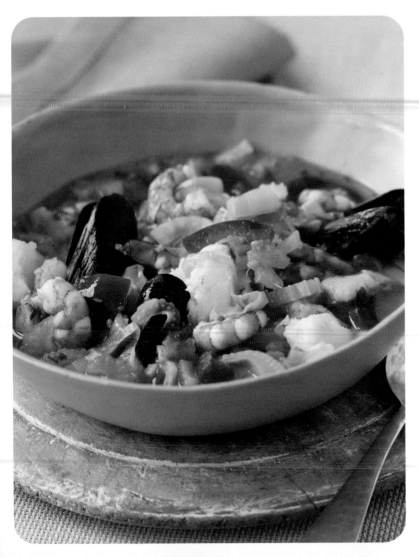

Chinese-style Fish

Preparation Time 5 minutes • Cooking Time 10 minutes • Serves 4 • Per Serving 150 calories,
3g fat (of which 1g saturates), 10g carbohydrate, 0.7g salt • Easy

2 tsp sunflower oil
1 small onion, finely chopped
1 green chilli, seeded and finely chopped (see Cook's Tips, page 38)
2 courgettes, thinly sliced

125g (4oz) frozen peas, thawed
350g (12oz) skinless haddock fillet, cut into bite-size pieces
2 tsp lemon juice
4 tbsp hoisin sauce
lime wedges to serve

1. Heat the oil in a large non-stick frying pan. Add the onion, chilli, courgettes and peas and stir-fry over a high heat for 5 minutes or until the onion and courgettes begin to soften.

2. Add the fish to the pan with the lemon juice, hoisin sauce and 150ml (¼ pint) water. Bring to the boil, then reduce the heat and simmer, uncovered, for 2–3 minutes until the fish is cooked through. Serve with lime wedges.

TRY SOMETHING DIFFERENT
There are plenty of alternatives to haddock: try sea bass, sea bream or gurnard.

Cod with Sweet Chilli Glaze

Preparation Time 10 minutes • Cooking Time 20 minutes • Serves 4 • Per Serving 193 calories,
1g fat (of which trace saturates), 13g carbohydrate, 0.7g salt • Easy

**1 red chilli, seeded and finely
    chopped (see Cook's Tips,
    page 38)**
2 tsp dark soy sauce
grated zest and juice of 1 lime
**¼ tsp ground allspice or 6 allspice
    berries, crushed**
50g (2oz) light muscovado sugar
**4 thick cod fillets, with skin, about
    175g (6oz) each**

**finely sliced red chilli, finely sliced
    lime zest and lime wedges to
    garnish**

FOR THE SAFFRON MASH
**900g (2lb) potatoes, roughly
    chopped**
a pinch of saffron threads
50g (2oz) butter
salt and ground black pepper

1. To make the saffron mash, cook the potatoes in lightly salted boiling water until tender. Meanwhile, soak the saffron in 2 tbsp boiling water. Drain the potatoes and mash with the butter, then beat in the saffron liquid. Season to taste with salt and pepper.

2. Meanwhile, preheat the grill or griddle pan until hot. Stir the chopped chilli, soy sauce, lime zest and juice, allspice and sugar together.

3. Grill the cod for about 1 minute on the flesh side. Turn skin side up and grill for 1 minute. Spoon the chilli glaze over the fish and grill for a further 2–3 minutes until the skin is crisp and golden.

4. Garnish with finely sliced chilli and lime zest and the lime wedges. Serve with the saffron mash.

**TRY SOMETHING
DIFFERENT**
*Use sea bass, gurnard, coley
(saithe) or pollack instead of the
cod.*

Crusted Trout

Preparation Time 10 minutes • Cooking Time 10–13 minutes • Serves 4 • Per Serving 259 calories, 15g fat (of which 3g saturates), 1g carbohydrate, 0.8g salt • Easy

1 tbsp sesame oil
1 tbsp soy sauce
juice of 1 lime
4 × 150g (5oz) trout fillets
2 tbsp sesame seeds
**lime wedges, herb salad and fennel
    to serve**

1. Preheat the grill. Put the oil into a bowl, add the soy sauce and lime juice and whisk together.

2. Put the trout fillets on a baking sheet, pour the sesame mixture over them and grill for 8–10 minutes. Sprinkle with the sesame seeds and grill for a further 2–3 minutes until the seeds are golden. Serve with lime wedges, a herb salad and some finely sliced fennel.

COOK'S TIP
Sesame seeds are deliciously nutty and highly nutritious. They are a valuable source of protein, good omega fats and vitamin E. Lightly toasted sesame seeds, crushed with a little salt and stirred into 1–2 tbsp olive oil, make an excellent dressing for cooked green beans, broccoli and carrots.

Trout with Apple & Watercress Salad

Preparation Time 15 minutes • Cooking Time 15–20 minutes • Serves 4 • Per Serving 320 calories, 12g fat (of which 1g saturates), 21g carbohydrate, 0.4g salt • Easy

4 × 150g (5oz) trout fillets
1 tbsp olive oil, plus extra to grease
250g (9oz) cooked baby new
   potatoes, cut into chunks
2 apples, cored and cut into chunks
4 cooked beetroot in natural juice,
   cut into chunks
150g (5oz) watercress
salt and ground black pepper

FOR THE DRESSING
1 tbsp extra virgin olive oil
juice of ½ lemon
2 tsp Dijon mustard
1 tbsp freshly chopped dill

1. Preheat the oven to 200°C (180°C fan oven) mark 6. Put each piece of fish on a piece of greased foil, brush the top of the fish with olive oil and season with salt and pepper. Scrunch the foil around the fish and roast for 15–20 minutes until the fish is cooked.

2. Put the potatoes, apples, beetroot and watercress into a large bowl and mix lightly.

3. Mix all the dressing ingredients together in a small bowl and season with salt and pepper. Add to the salad and toss through, then serve with the fish.

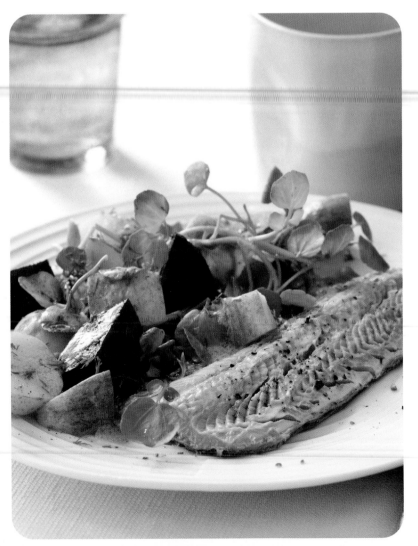

Crispy Crumbed Fish

Preparation Time 5 minutes • Cooking Time 10–15 minutes • Serves 4 • Per Serving 171 calories,
1g fat (of which trace saturates), 10g carbohydrate, 0.8g salt • Easy

50g (2oz) fresh breadcrumbs
a small handful of freshly chopped
   flat-leafed parsley
2 tbsp capers, chopped
grated zest of 1 lemon
4 haddock or pollack fillets, about
   150g (5oz) each

½ tbsp Dijon mustard
juice of ½ lemon
salt and ground black pepper
new potatoes and mixed salad
   to serve

1. Preheat the oven to 180°C (160°C fan oven) mark 4. Put the breadcrumbs into a bowl with the parsley, capers and lemon zest. Mix well, then set aside.

2. Put the fish fillets on a baking tray. Mix the mustard and half the lemon juice in a bowl with a little salt and pepper, then spread over the top of each piece of fish. Spoon the breadcrumb mixture on top – don't worry if some falls off.

3. Cook in the oven for 10–15 minutes until the fish is cooked and the breadcrumbs are golden. Pour the remaining lemon juice over the top and serve with new potatoes and a mixed salad.

Quick Fish & Chips

Preparation Time 15 minutes • Cooking Time 12 minutes • Serves 2 • Per Serving 1186 calories, 79g fat (of which 18g saturates), 73g carbohydrate, 3.2g salt • Easy

4 litres (7 pints) sunflower oil for deep-frying
125g (4oz) self-raising flour
¼ tsp baking powder
¼ tsp salt
1 medium egg
150ml (¼ pint) sparkling mineral water
2 hake fillets, about 125g (4oz) each
450g (1lb) Desirée potatoes, cut into 1cm (½in) chips
salt, vinegar and garlic mayonnaise to serve

1. Heat the oil in a deep-fryer to 190°C (test by frying a small cube of bread – it should brown in 20 seconds).

2. Whiz the flour, baking powder, salt, egg and water in a food processor until combined into a batter. Remove the blade from the food processor. Alternatively, put the ingredients into a bowl and beat everything together until smooth. Drop one of the fish fillets into the batter to coat it.

3. Put half the chips in the deep-fryer, then add the battered fish. Fry for 6 minutes or until just cooked, then remove and drain well on kitchen paper. Keep warm if not serving immediately.

4. Drop the remaining fillet into the batter to coat, then repeat step 3 with the remaining chips. Serve with salt, vinegar and garlic mayonnaise.

Thai Fishcakes with Chilli Mayo

Preparation Time 25 minutes • Cooking Time 8–10 minutes • Serves 4 • Per Serving 554 calories, 44g fat (of which 6g saturates), 17g carbohydrate, 1.3g salt • Easy

1 bunch of spring onions

2.5cm (1in) piece fresh root ginger, peeled and roughly chopped

1 lemongrass stalk, roughly chopped

20g pack fresh coriander

½ red chilli, seeded (see Cook's Tips, page 38), plus strips of red chilli to garnish

1 tsp Thai fish sauce (optional)

150ml (¼ pint) mayonnaise

75g (3oz) fresh white breadcrumbs

225g (8oz) haddock

225g (8oz) cooked and peeled prawns

oil for frying

2 tbsp Thai sweet chilli sauce

20g pack fresh basil, roughly chopped

1 fat garlic clove, crushed (optional)

2 limes, cut into wedges, and 120g bag baby leaf spinach to serve

1. Put the spring onions, ginger, lemongrass, coriander, chilli and fish sauce, if using, into a food processor and whiz to a rough paste. Add 3 tbsp mayonnaise, the breadcrumbs, haddock and prawns and whiz for 5 seconds.

2. With wet hands, shape the mixture into eight patties, each about 5cm (2in) in diameter.

3. Heat a drizzle of oil in a non-stick frying pan. Fry the patties, in two batches, for 3–4 minutes on each side until crisp and golden.

4. Mix the sweet chilli sauce, basil and garlic, if using, into the remaining mayonnaise.

5. Serve the fishcakes garnished with red chilli strips, with lime wedges, the chilli mayo and spinach leaves.

Simple Smoked Haddock

Preparation Time 10 minutes • Cooking Time 10 minutes • Serves 4 • Per Serving 217 calories, 9g fat (of which 4g saturates), 1g carbohydrate, 3.4g salt • **Easy**

25g (1oz) unsalted butter
1 tbsp olive oil
1 garlic clove, thinly sliced
4 thick smoked haddock or cod fillets, about 175g (6oz) each
a small handful of freshly chopped parsley (optional)
finely grated zest of 1 small lemon, plus lemon wedges to serve (optional)
romanesco, cauliflower or broccoli to serve

1. Heat the butter, oil and garlic in a large non-stick pan over a high heat until the mixture starts to foam and sizzle. Put the fish into the pan, skin side down, and fry for 10 minutes – this will give a golden crust underneath the fish.

2. Turn the fish over. Scatter the parsley, if using, and lemon zest over each fillet, then fry for a further 30 seconds.

3. Put a cooked fillet on each of four warmed plates and spoon some of the buttery juices over them. Serve with lemon wedges, if using, and steamed romanesco, cauliflower or broccoli.

COOK'S TIP
Smoked fish is quite salty so always taste the sauce before seasoning with any extra salt.

Pesto Cod with Butter Beans

Preparation Time 5 minutes • Cooking Time 15 minutes • Serves 4 • Per Serving 403 calories, 16g fat (of which 3g saturates), 24g carbohydrate, 2.5g salt • Easy

4 cod fillets, about 150g (5oz) each

4 tbsp red pepper pesto

2 tbsp olive oil

2 × 400g cans butter beans, drained and rinsed

2 garlic cloves, crushed

225g (8oz) fresh spinach

lemon juice

salt and ground black pepper

lemon juice to serve

1. Preheat the grill to medium. Spread each cod fillet evenly with 1 tbsp pesto and grill for 10–15 minutes until the flesh is opaque and just cooked.

2. Meanwhile, heat the oil in a pan and add the butter beans and garlic. Cook for 10 minutes, stirring occasionally and mashing the beans lightly as they warm through. Season with salt and pepper.

3. About 2–3 minutes before serving, add the spinach to the pan and allow it to wilt. Spoon the butter beans on to four warmed plates and top with the cod and any juices from grilling. Squeeze a little lemon juice over each piece of fish and serve immediately.

Grilled Sardines with Harissa

Preparation Time 10 minutes • Cooking Time 10–20 minutes • Serves 2 • Per Serving 292 calories,
21g fat (of which 4g saturates), 2g carbohydrate, 0.3g salt • Easy

1 garlic clove, crushed

2 tbsp olive oil

1–2 tsp harissa paste

4 whole sardines

salt and ground black pepper

**tomato salad, watercress and lime
    wedges to serve**

1. Preheat the grill to high. Put the garlic in a bowl. Add the oil and harissa, season to taste with salt and pepper and mix well.

2. Slash the sardines a couple of times on each side, then brush the harissa and oil mixture all over them. Grill for 5–10 minutes on each side until cooked through.

3. Serve with tomato salad and watercress, with lime wedges to squeeze over the sardines.

COOK'S TIP

Oily fish such as sardines are one of the best sources of heart-protecting omega-3 oils. Eat them at least once a week. Fresh Cornish sardines, when they are available, are a treat and are cheap. Look out for them at your fishmonger's or on the fresh fish counter at the supermarket.

Peppered Mackerel

Preparation Time 10 minutes • Cooking Time 15 minutes • Serves 4 • Per Serving 764 calories,
63g fat (of which 22g saturates), 1g carbohydrate, 0.4g salt • Easy

4 tsp whole mixed peppercorns
4 fresh mackerel, gutted, about
    250g (9oz) each
1 tbsp sunflower oil
200ml (7fl oz) crème fraîche
lemon wedges to garnish
asparagus and sugarsnap peas
    to serve

1. Lightly crush 2 tsp peppercorns using a pestle and mortar. Sprinkle one side of each mackerel with half the crushed peppercorns.

2. Heat the oil in a frying pan over a medium-high heat. Add the fish, peppered side down, and cook for 5–7 minutes. Sprinkle the mackerel with the remaining crushed peppercorns, turn the fish over and continue to fry for 5–7 minutes until cooked (see Cook's Tips). Remove and keep warm.

3. Wipe out the pan, add the crème fraîche and bring to the boil. Stir in the remaining whole peppercorns. (If the sauce becomes too thick, add some boiling water.)

4. To serve, spoon the sauce over the mackerel, garnish with lemon wedges and serve with asparagus and sugarsnap peas.

COOK'S TIPS
• *If the mackerel are large, make three shallow slashes on either side of the fish.*
• *To test whether the fish is cooked, prise the flesh from the backbone with a knife: it should be opaque and come away easily.*

Tuna Melt Pizza

Preparation Time 5 minutes • Cooking Time 10–12 minutes • Serves 4 • Per Serving 688 calories, 26g fat (of which 9g saturates), 72g carbohydrate, 3.5g salt • Easy

2 large pizza bases
4 tbsp sun-dried tomato pesto
2 × 185g cans tuna, drained
50g can anchovies, drained and chopped
125g (4oz) mature Cheddar, grated
rocket to serve

1. Preheat the oven to 220°C (200°C fan oven) mark 7. Spread each pizza base with 2 tbsp sun-dried tomato pesto. Top each with half the tuna, half the anchovies and half the grated cheese.

2. Put on to a baking sheet and cook in the oven for 10–12 minutes until the cheese has melted. Sprinkle with rocket to serve.

TRY SOMETHING DIFFERENT

Mozzarella & Tomato Pizza
Spread the pizza bases with 4 tbsp pesto and top with 125g (4oz) chopped sunblush tomatoes and 2 x 125g sliced mozzarella balls. Cook, then serve topped with a handful of baby spinach leaves.

Ham & Pineapple Pizza
Spread the pizza bases with 4 tbsp tomato pasta sauce. Top with a 225g can drained unsweetened pineapple chunks, 125g (4oz) diced ham and 125g (4oz) grated Gruyère.

Simple Salmon Pasta

Preparation Time 2 minutes • Cooking Time 8 minutes • Serves 4 • Per Serving 630 calories, 13g fat (of which 6g saturates), 101g carbohydrate, 2.7g salt • Easy

500g (1lb 2oz) linguine pasta
a little olive oil
1 fat garlic clove, crushed
200ml (7fl oz) half-fat crème fraîche
225g (8oz) hot-smoked salmon, flaked
200g (7oz) peas
2 handfuls of fresh basil, roughly torn, to garnish
salt and ground black pepper

1. Cook the pasta in a large pan of lightly salted boiling water according to the pack instructions, then drain, reserving a couple of tablespoons of the cooking water.

2. Meanwhile, heat the oil in a large pan, add the garlic and fry gently until golden. Add the crème fraîche, salmon and peas and stir in. Cook for 1–2 minutes until warmed through, then add the reserved water from the pasta.

3. Toss the pasta in the sauce, season with salt and pepper and serve garnished with the torn basil.

COOK'S TIP
Adding the reserved pasta cooking water stops the pasta absorbing too much of the crème fraîche.

Stir-fried Salmon & Broccoli

Preparation Time 10 minutes • Cooking Time 5–6 minutes • Serves 2 • Per Serving 90 calories,
4g fat (of which 1g saturates), 9g carbohydrate, 2.7g salt • Easy

2 tsp sesame oil
1 red pepper, seeded and thinly
sliced
½ red chilli, seeded and thinly
sliced (see Cook's Tips, page 38)
1 garlic clove, crushed
125g (4oz) broccoli florets
2 spring onions, sliced
2 salmon fillets, about 125g (4oz)
each, cut into strips
1 tsp Thai fish sauce
2 tsp soy sauce
wholewheat noodles to serve

1. Heat the oil in a wok or large
frying pan. Add the red pepper,
chilli, garlic, broccoli florets and
spring onions and stir-fry over a
high heat for 3–4 minutes.

2. Add the salmon, fish sauce and
soy sauce and cook for 2 minutes,
stirring gently. Serve immediately
with wholewheat noodles.

Five-minute Stir-fry

Preparation Time 2 minutes • Cooking Time 5 minutes • Serves 2 • Per Serving 170 calories, 7g fat (of which 1g saturates), 11g carbohydrate, 1.6g salt • Easy

1 tbsp sesame oil

175g (6oz) raw peeled tiger prawns, deveined (see Cook's Tip)

50ml (2fl oz) ready-made sweet chilli and ginger sauce

225g (8oz) ready-prepared mixed stir-fry vegetables, such as sliced courgettes, broccoli and green beans

1. Heat the oil in a large wok or frying pan, add the prawns and sweet chilli and ginger sauce and stir-fry for 2 minutes.

2. Add the mixed vegetables and stir-fry for a further 2–3 minutes until the prawns are cooked and the vegetables are heated through. Serve immediately.

TRY SOMETHING DIFFERENT

Instead of prawns, try chicken cut into strips: stir-fry for 5 minutes in step 1.

COOK'S TIP

To devein prawns, pull off the head and discard (or put to one side and use later for making stock). Using pointed scissors, cut through the soft shell on the belly side. Prise off the shell, leaving the tail attached. (The shell can also be used later for making stock.) Using a small sharp knife, make a shallow cut along the back of the prawn. Using the point of the knife, remove and discard the black vein (the intestinal tract) that runs along the back of the prawn.

Ginger, Leek & Prawn Stir-fry

Preparation Time 10 minutes • Cooking Time 15 minutes • Serves 4 • Per Serving 152 calories,
3g fat (of which 1g saturates), 10g carbohydrate, 1.2g salt • Easy

2 tsp olive oil
1 bunch of spring onions, chopped
1 garlic clove, crushed
2.5cm (1in) piece fresh root ginger,
**   peeled and grated**
3 leeks, trimmed and roughly
**   chopped**
1 red pepper, seeded and roughly
**   chopped**

400g (14oz) cooked prawns
1 tbsp tamari (wheat-free Japanese
**   soy sauce)**
2 tsp tomato purée, diluted in
**   1 tbsp water**
1 tsp runny honey
ground black pepper
rice or quinoa to serve

1. Heat the oil in a pan, add the
spring onions, garlic, ginger and
2 tbsp water and fry for 2 minutes
over a medium heat. Add the leeks
and red pepper and stir-fry for
10 minutes or until softened.

2. Add the prawns, tamari, tomato
purée and honey to the pan.
Season with pepper and cook for
30 seconds to 1 minute, stirring.
Serve with rice or quinoa.

**TRY SOMETHING
DIFFERENT**
*Use scallops instead of the prawns.
Alternatively, use any firm-textured
white fish, such as monkfish,
discarding the skin and cutting
the fish into small cubes.*

Prawn & Peanut Noodles

Preparation Time 10 minutes, plus soaking • Serves 4 • Per Serving 579 calories, 24g fat (of which 7g saturates), 67g carbohydrate, 0.7g salt • Easy

300g (11oz) straight-to-wok noodles
360g pack stir-fry vegetables
4 tbsp coconut cream
4 tbsp smooth peanut butter
1 tbsp Thai red or green curry paste
juice of ½ lime
225g (8oz) cooked and peeled king prawns
a small handful of freshly chopped coriander
25g (1oz) peanuts, chopped

1. Put the noodles and stir-fry vegetables into a large bowl or wok and cover with boiling water. Cover with clingfilm and leave for 5 minutes.

2. Meanwhile, mix the coconut cream with the peanut butter, curry paste and lime juice in a bowl.

3. Drain the noodles and vegetables in a colander. Put back into the bowl and toss with the prawns, coriander and half the dressing. Sprinkle with the peanuts and serve with the remaining dressing.

COOK'S TIP

Ready-prepared stir-fry vegetables make this extra-quick, but if you can't find them, try a mixture of three or four of the following: strips of red, orange or yellow peppers, baby sweetcorn, mangetouts or sugarsnaps, carrots cut into matchsticks, bean sprouts.

Penne with Smoked Salmon

Preparation Time 5 minutes • Cooking Time 10–15 minutes • Serves 4 • Per Serving 432 calories,
11g fat (of which 6g saturates), 67g carbohydrate, 1.7g salt • Easy

**350g (12oz) penne or other short
tubular pasta**
200ml (7fl oz) half-fat crème fraîche
**150g (5oz) smoked salmon, roughly
chopped**
20g (¾oz) fresh dill, finely chopped
salt and ground black pepper
lemon wedges to serve (optional)

1. Cook the pasta in a large pan
of lightly salted boiling water
according to the pack instructions.
Drain.

2. Meanwhile, put the crème
fraîche into a large bowl. Add the
smoked salmon and dill, season
well with salt and pepper and mix
together. Gently stir into the drained
penne and serve immediately with
lemon wedges, if you like, to
squeeze over the salmon and pasta.

Prawn & Vegetable Pilau

Preparation Time 10 minutes • Cooking Time 15–20 minutes • Serves 4 • Per Serving 360 calories, 5g fat (of which 1g saturates), 61g carbohydrate, 1.8g salt • Easy

250g (9oz) long-grain rice

1 broccoli head, broken into florets

150g (5oz) baby sweetcorn, halved

200g (7oz) sugarsnap peas

1 red pepper, seeded and sliced into thin strips

400g (14oz) cooked and peeled king prawns

FOR THE DRESSING

1 tbsp sesame oil

5cm (2in) piece fresh root ginger, peeled and grated

juice of 1 lime

1–2 tbsp light soy sauce

1. Put the rice into a large wide pan – it needs to be really big, as you'll be cooking the rice and steaming the vegetables on top, then tossing it all together. Add 600ml (1 pint) boiling water. Cover and bring to the boil, then reduce the heat to low and cook the rice according to the pack instructions.

2. About 10 minutes before the end of the rice cooking time, add the broccoli, corn, sugarsnaps and red pepper. Stir well, then cover the pan and cook until the vegetables and rice are just tender.

3. Meanwhile, put the prawns into a bowl. Add the sesame oil, ginger, lime and soy sauce. Mix the prawns and dressing into the cooked vegetables and rice and toss well. Serve immediately.

COOK'S TIP

The word 'pilau', or 'pilaf', comes from the Persian 'pilaw'. The dish consists of rice flavoured with spices, to which vegetables, poultry, meat, fish or shellfish are added.

Simple Fried Rice

Preparation Time 5 minutes • Cooking Time 15–20 minutes • Serves 4 • Per Serving 339 calories, 11g fat (of which 2g saturates), 37g carbohydrate, 0.4g salt • Easy

150g (5oz) long-grain rice
2 tbsp sesame oil
3 medium eggs, lightly beaten
250g (9oz) frozen petits pois
250g (9oz) cooked and peeled prawns

1. Cook the rice in boiling water for about 10 minutes or according to the pack instructions. Drain well.

2. Heat 1 tsp oil in a large non-stick frying pan. Pour in half the beaten eggs and tilt the pan around over the heat for about 1 minute until the egg is set. Tip the omelette on to a warm plate. Repeat with another 1 tsp oil and the remaining beaten egg to make another omelette. Tip on to another warm plate.

3. Add the remaining oil to the pan and stir in the rice and peas. Stir-fry for 2–3 minutes until the peas are cooked. Stir in the prawns.

4. Roll up the omelettes, roughly chop one-third of one, then slice the remainder into strips. Add the chopped omelette to the rice, peas and prawns and cook for 1–2 minutes until heated through. Divide the fried rice among four bowls, top with the sliced omelette and serve immediately.

Quick Pad Thai

Preparation Time 12 minutes, plus soaking • Cooking Time 8 minutes • Serves 4 • Per Serving 451 calories,
13g fat (of which 3g saturates), 56g carbohydrate, 2.6g salt • Easy

250g (9oz) wide ribbon rice noodles
3 tbsp satay and sweet chilli pesto
(see Cook's Tips)
125g (4oz) mangetouts, thinly
sliced
125g (4oz) sugarsnap peas, thinly
sliced
3 medium eggs, beaten

3 tbsp chilli soy sauce, plus extra
to serve (see Cook's Tips)
250g (9oz) cooked and peeled tiger
prawns
25g (1oz) dry-roasted peanuts,
roughly crushed
lime wedges to serve (optional)

1. Put the noodles into a heatproof bowl, cover with boiling water and soak for 4 minutes until softened. Drain, rinse under cold water and set aside.

2. Heat a wok or large frying pan until hot, add the chilli pesto and stir-fry for 1 minute. Add the mangetouts and sugarsnap peas and cook for a further 2 minutes. Tip into a bowl. Put the pan back on the heat, add the eggs and cook, stirring, for 1 minute.

3. Add the soy sauce, prawns and noodles to the pan. Toss well and cook for 3 minutes or until piping hot. Return the vegetables to the pan and cook for a further 1 minute until heated through, then sprinkle with the peanuts. Serve with extra soy sauce, and lime wedges to squeeze over the pad Thai, if you like.

COOK'S TIPS
• *If you can't find satay and sweet chilli pesto, substitute 2 tbsp peanut butter and 1 tbsp sweet chilli sauce.*
• *Chilli soy sauce can be replaced with 2 tbsp light soy sauce and ½ red chilli, finely chopped (see Cook's Tips, page 38).*

Mussel & Potato Stew

Preparation Time 15 minutes • Cooking Time 15 minutes • Serves 4 • Per Serving 470 calories,
23g fat (of which 11g saturates), 42g carbohydrate, 2.8g salt • Easy

25g (1oz) butter
200g (7oz) rindless back bacon
  rashers, cut into strips
700g (1½lb) white potatoes, cut into
  large chunks
200g can sweetcorn, drained

1kg (2¼lb) mussels, scrubbed,
  rinsed and beards removed (see
  Cook's Tip)
150ml (¼ pint) single cream
1 tbsp freshly chopped flat-leafed
  parsley
salt and ground black pepper

1. Melt the butter in a large pan, add the bacon and cook, stirring, until the strips separate. Add the potatoes and 150ml (¼ pint) water and season lightly with salt and pepper. Cover with a tight-fitting lid and cook for 10 minutes or until the potatoes are almost tender.

2. Add the sweetcorn and mussels to the pan, cover and bring to the boil, then reduce the heat and simmer for 2–3 minutes until the mussels open; discard any mussels that don't open. Add the cream and chopped parsley and serve immediately.

COOK'S TIP
To make sure mussels are safe to eat, check them carefully for cracks and split shells before cooking. Discard these, and any that do not close when tapped sharply. Any mussels that remain closed after cooking should also be thrown away.

Salmon & Bulgur Wheat Pilau

Preparation Time 5 minutes • Cooking Time 20 minutes • Serves 4 • Per Serving 323 calories, 11g fat (of which 2g saturates), 30g carbohydrate, 1.5g salt • Easy

1 tbsp olive oil
1 onion, chopped
175g (6oz) bulgur wheat
450ml (¾ pint) vegetable stock
400g can pink salmon, drained and
**   flaked**
125g (4oz) spinach, roughly
**   chopped**
225g (8oz) frozen peas
zest and juice of 1 lemon
salt and ground black pepper

1. Heat the oil in a large pan, add the onion and cook until softened. Stir in the bulgur wheat to coat in the oil, then stir in the stock and bring to the boil. Cover, reduce the heat and simmer for 10–15 minutes until the stock has been fully absorbed.

2. Stir in the salmon, spinach, peas and lemon juice and cook until the spinach has wilted and the salmon and peas are heated through. Season to taste with salt and pepper and sprinkle with lemon zest before serving.

TRY SOMETHING DIFFERENT
Instead of salmon, use 200g (7oz) cooked peeled prawns and 200g (7oz) cherry tomatoes.

Salmon & Coconut Curry

Preparation Time 2 minutes • Cooking Time 18 minutes • Serves 4 • Per Serving 276 calories, 19g fat (of which 3g saturates), 8g carbohydrate, 0.6g salt • Easy

1 tbsp olive oil

1 red onion, sliced

2 tbsp tikka masala curry paste

4 × 100g (3½oz) salmon steaks

400ml can coconut milk

juice of 1 lime

a handful of fresh coriander,
   roughly chopped

TO SERVE

lime wedges

boiled rice

1. Heat the oil in a pan. Add the onion and cook over a medium heat for 10 minutes until soft.

2. Add the curry paste to the pan and cook for 1 minute to warm the spices. Add the fish and cook for 2 minutes, turning it once to coat it in the spices.

3. Pour in the coconut milk and bring to the boil, then reduce the heat and simmer for 5 minutes or until the fish is cooked through.

4. Pour the lime juice over the fish and sprinkle with coriander. Serve with lime wedges to squeeze over the fish, and boiled rice to soak up the creamy sauce.

FOOD FOR FRIENDS

Chicken with Oyster Sauce

Preparation Time 10 minutes • Cooking Time about 18 minutes • Serves 4 • Per Serving 344 calories, 23g fat (of which 3g saturates), 7g carbohydrate, 1.1g salt • Easy

6 tbsp vegetable oil

450g (1lb) boneless, skinless chicken breasts, cut into bite-size pieces

3 tbsp oyster sauce

1 tbsp dark soy sauce

100ml (3½fl oz) chicken stock

2 tsp lemon juice

1 garlic clove, thinly sliced

6–8 large flat mushrooms, about 250g (9oz) total weight, sliced

125g (4oz) mangetouts

1 tsp cornflour mixed with 1 tbsp water

1 tbsp toasted sesame oil

salt and ground black pepper

rice to serve

1. Heat 3 tbsp vegetable oil in a wok or large frying pan. Add the chicken and cook over a high heat, stirring continuously for 2–3 minutes until lightly browned. Remove the chicken with a slotted spoon and drain on kitchen paper.

2. Mix the oyster sauce with the soy sauce, stock and lemon juice. Add the chicken and mix thoroughly.

3. Heat the remaining vegetable oil in the pan over a high heat and stir-fry the garlic for about 30 seconds. Add the mushrooms and cook for 1 minute. Add the chicken mixture, cover and simmer for 2 minutes.

4. Stir in the mangetouts and cook for a further 2–3 minutes. Remove the pan from the heat and stir in the cornflour mixture. Put the pan back on the heat, add the sesame oil and stir until the sauce has thickened. Season with salt and pepper and serve immediately with rice.

Chicken with Wine & Capers

Preparation Time 5 minutes • Cooking Time 25 minutes • Serves 4 • Per Serving 234 calories, 10g fat (of which 5g saturates), trace carbohydrate, 0.3g salt • Easy

1 tbsp olive oil
15g (½oz) butter
4 small skinless chicken breasts
lemon wedges to garnish
boiled rice to serve

FOR THE WINE AND CAPER SAUCE
125ml (4fl oz) white wine
3 tbsp capers, rinsed and drained
juice of 1 lemon
15g (½oz) butter
1 tbsp freshly chopped flat-leafed parsley

1. Heat the oil and butter in a frying pan over a medium heat. Add the chicken breasts and fry for 10–12 minutes on each side until cooked through. Transfer to a warm plate, cover and keep warm.

2. To make the sauce, add the wine and capers to the same pan. Bring to the boil, then reduce the heat and simmer for 2–3 minutes until the wine is reduced by half. Add the lemon juice and butter and stir in the parsley.

3. Divide the chicken among four warmed plates, pour the sauce over the chicken, garnish each serving with a lemon wedge and serve immediately with boiled rice.

Chicken Tarragon

Preparation Time 15 minutes • Cooking Time about 15 minutes • Serves 4 • Per Serving 571 calories, 40g fat (of which 22g saturates), 7g carbohydrate, 0.2g salt • Easy

4 x 125g (4oz) chicken breasts,
   cut into bite-size pieces
25g (1oz) plain flour
2 tbsp olive oil
250g (9oz) chestnut mushrooms,
   sliced
150ml (5fl oz) white wine
300ml (½ pint) crème fraîche
½ tbsp Dijon mustard
2 tbsp freshly chopped tarragon
a large handful of spinach
salt and freshly ground black
   pepper
crusty bread to serve

1. Put the chicken into a bowl and sprinkle over the flour and some seasoning. Mix together. Heat half of the oil in a large frying pan over a medium-high heat. Brown the chicken for 5 minutes until golden – do this in batches if necessary to stop the chicken from sweating. Remove from the pan and put to one side.

2. Add the remaining oil to the pan and fry the mushrooms for 3–5 minutes until nearly cooked through. Put the chicken and any juices back into the pan. Pour over the wine and simmer for 2 minutes, then stir in the crème fraîche, mustard and most of the tarragon. Bring to the boil, reduce the heat and simmer for 5 minutes or until the chicken is cooked through.

3. Stir in the spinach and check the seasoning. Sprinkle over the remaining tarragon and serve with crusty bread to mop up the juices.

Mediterranean Chicken

Preparation Time 5 minutes • Cooking Time 20 minutes • Serves 4 • Per Serving 223 calories,
7g fat (of which 1g saturates), 3g carbohydrate, 0.2g salt • Easy

1 red pepper, seeded and chopped
2 tbsp capers
2 tbsp freshly chopped rosemary
2 tbsp olive oil
**4 skinless chicken breasts, about
    125g (4oz) each**
salt and ground black pepper
rice or new potatoes to serve

1. Preheat the oven to 200°C (180°C fan oven) mark 6. Put the red pepper into a bowl with the capers, rosemary and oil. Season with salt and pepper and mix well.

2. Put the chicken breasts into an ovenproof dish and spoon the pepper mixture over the top. Roast for 15–20 minutes until the chicken is cooked through and the topping is hot. Serve with rice or new potatoes.

TRY SOMETHING DIFFERENT
Use chopped black olives instead of the capers.

Garlic & Thyme Chicken

Preparation Time 10 minutes • Cooking Time 10–15 minutes • Serves 4 • Per Serving 135 calories, 6g fat (of which 1g saturates), trace carbohydrate, 0.2g salt • Easy

2 garlic cloves, crushed
2 tbsp freshly chopped thyme leaves
2 tbsp olive oil
4 chicken thighs
salt and ground black pepper

1. Preheat the barbecue or grill. Mix the garlic with the thyme and oil in a large bowl. Season with salt and pepper.

2. Using a sharp knife, make two or three slits in each chicken thigh. Put the chicken into the bowl and toss to coat thoroughly. Barbecue or grill for 5–7 minutes on each side until golden and cooked through.

Moroccan Spiced Chicken Kebabs

Preparation Time 10 minutes, plus marinating • Cooking Time 10–12 minutes • Serves 4 • Per Serving 190 calories, 7g fat (of which 1g saturates), 1g carbohydrate, 0.2g salt • Easy

2 tbsp olive oil

15g (½oz) flat-leafed parsley

1 garlic clove

½ tsp paprika

1 tsp ground cumin

zest and juice of 1 lemon

4 skinless chicken breasts, cut into bite-size chunks

salt

shredded lettuce, sliced cucumber and tomatoes, and lime wedges to serve

1. Put the oil into a blender and add the parsley, garlic, paprika, cumin, lemon zest and juice and a pinch of salt. Whiz to make a paste.

2. Put the chicken into a medium-sized shallow dish and rub in the spice paste. Leave to marinate for at least 20 minutes. Preheat the grill to high. Soak some wooden skewers in water.

3. Thread the marinated chicken on to the skewers and grill for 10–12 minutes, turning every now and then, until the meat is cooked through. Serve with shredded lettuce, sliced cucumber and tomatoes, and lime wedges.

TRY SOMETHING DIFFERENT
Instead of chicken, use 700g (1½lb) lean lamb fillet or leg of lamb, cut into chunks.

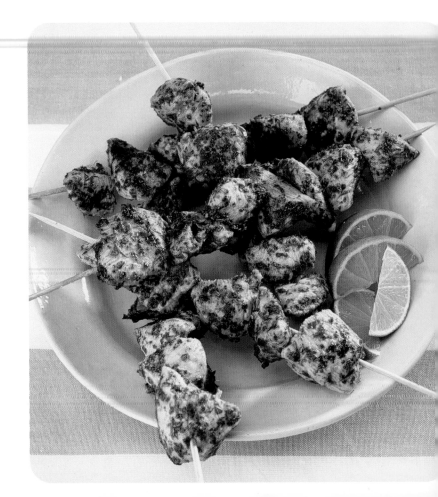

Pork Steaks with Sage & Parma Ham

Preparation Time 5 minutes • Cooking Time 10 minutes • Serves 4 • Per Serving 328 calories, 20g fat, (of which 9g saturates), 4g carbohydrate, 0.8g salt • Easy

4 pork shoulder steaks, about 150g (5oz) each
4 thin slices Parma ham or pancetta
6 sage leaves
1 tbsp oil
150ml (¼ pint) pure unsweetened apple juice
50g (2oz) chilled butter, diced
squeeze of lemon juice
ground black pepper
steamed cabbage or kale and mashed sweet potatoes to serve

1. Put the pork steaks on a board. Lay a slice of Parma ham or pancetta and a sage leaf on each pork steak, then secure to the meat with a wooden cocktail stick. Season with pepper.

2. Heat the oil in a large heavy-based frying pan and fry the pork for 3–4 minutes on each side until golden brown.

3. Pour the apple juice into the pan, stirring and scraping up the sediment from the base of the pan. Let the liquid bubble until reduced by half. Lift the pork out on to a warmed plate.

4. Return the pan to the heat, add the butter and swirl until melted into the pan juices. Add lemon juice to taste, then pour the sauce over the pork. Serve with cabbage or curly kale and sweet potatoes.

Pork with Artichokes & Beans

Preparation Time 10 minutes • Cooking Time 8 minutes • Serves 4 • Per Serving 473 calories,
36g fat (of which 6g saturates), 17g carbohydrate, 3.7g salt • Easy

2 tbsp vegetable oil
2 pork fillets, about 275g (10oz)
    each, cut into 1cm (½in) slices
2 tbsp freshly chopped thyme
    leaves
8 tbsp olive oil
400g can artichoke hearts, drained,
    rinsed and quartered

400g can flageolet beans, drained
    and rinsed
185g jar pitted green olives,
    drained and rinsed
juice of 1 lemon
salt and ground black pepper

1. Heat the vegetable oil in a
frying pan over a medium heat and
fry the pork for 2 minutes on each
side. Add the thyme and season
with salt and pepper.

2. Meanwhile, heat the olive oil
in a separate pan over a medium
heat. Add the artichokes and
beans and cook for 3–4 minutes.
Add the olives and lemon juice
and season with pepper

3. Put the pork on top of the
artichokes, beans and olives and
serve immediately.

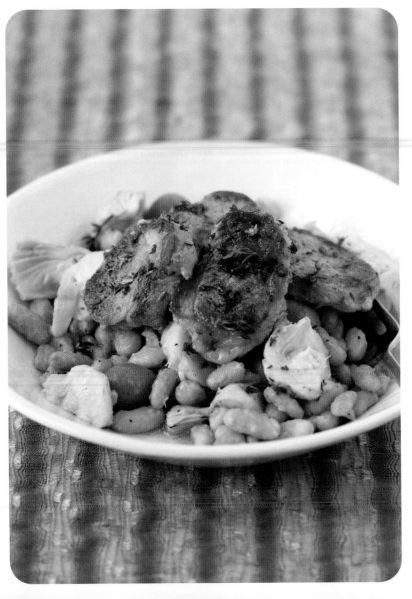

Spiced Pork with Lemon Pasta

Preparation Time 10 minutes • Cooking Time 12 minutes • Serves 6 • Per Serving 733 calories, 44g fat (of which 28g saturates), 71g carbohydrate, 1.8g salt • Easy

8 thick pork sausages
500g (1lb 2oz) pasta shells or other shapes
100ml (3½fl oz) chicken stock
grated zest of 1 lemon
juice of ½ lemon
a large pinch of dried chilli flakes

300ml (½ pint) half-fat crème fraîche
2 tbsp freshly chopped flat-leafed parsley
salt and ground black pepper
25g (1oz) freshly grated Parmesan to serve

1. Remove the skin from the sausages and pinch the meat into small pieces. Heat a non-stick frying pan over a medium heat. When hot, add the sausagemeat and cook for 5 minutes, stirring occasionally, or until cooked through and browned.

2. Meanwhile, cook the pasta in a large pan of lightly salted boiling water according to the pack instructions until al dente.

3. Add the stock to the sausagemeat, bring to the boil and let bubble, stirring, for 2–3 minutes until the liquid has reduced right down. Add the lemon zest and juice, chilli flakes and crème fraîche. Season well with salt and pepper. Continue to cook for 3–4 minutes until reduced and thickened slightly.

4. Drain the pasta and return to the pan. Stir the parsley into the sauce and toss with the pasta. Serve immediately, with grated Parmesan.

Fennel Pork with Cabbage & Apple

Preparation Time 10 minutes • Cooking Time 6–10 minutes • Serves 4 • Per Serving 276 calories,
12g fat (of which 3g saturates), 9g carbohydrate, 0.3g salt • Easy

2 tbsp olive oil
½ tbsp fennel seeds, crushed
1 tbsp freshly chopped sage
4 lean pork medallions, 125g (4oz)
  each
½ small red cabbage, shredded
450g (1lb) purple sprouting
  broccoli, tough ends removed
1 apple, cored and sliced into rings
salt and ground black pepper

1. Put 1 tbsp oil into a large shallow bowl. Add the fennel seeds and sage, season with salt and pepper and mix well. Add the pork and rub the mixture into the meat.

2. Heat the remaining oil in a wok or large frying pan and stir-fry the cabbage and broccoli for 6–8 minutes until starting to char.

3. Meanwhile, heat a non-stick griddle until hot and fry the pork for 2–3 minutes on each side until cooked through. Remove and set aside. Add the apple rings to the pan and griddle for 1–2 minutes on each side until starting to char and caramelise. Serve with the pork and vegetables.

Lamb with Orange & Mint

Preparation Time 10 minutes • Cooking Time 20 minutes • Serves 4 • Per Serving 451 calories,
32g fat (of which 11g saturates), 6g carbohydrate, 1.1g salt • Easy

4 tbsp olive oil

**4 lamb steaks, about 700g (1½lb)
total weight**

**185g jar chargrilled sweet red
peppers, drained and roughly
chopped**

50g (2oz) black olives

1 orange

juice of 1 lemon

**1 small bunch of mint, roughly
chopped**

salt and ground black pepper

1. Heat 2 tbsp oil in a large non-stick frying pan. Brown the lamb in the hot oil, turning occasionally, until the meat has formed a deep golden-brown crust all over.

2. Reduce the heat and add the peppers and olives to the pan. Chop up the orange, squeeze the juice directly into the pan and add the orange pieces for extra flavour. Add the lemon juice and the remaining oil.

3. Simmer for 5 minutes, stirring to break down the peppers a little. Stir the mint into the pan. Season to taste with salt and pepper and serve.

**TRY SOMETHING
DIFFERENT**

*Add a handful of shredded spinach
with the mint.*

Lamb with Spicy Couscous

Preparation Time 10 minutes • Cooking Time 15 minutes • Serves 4 • Per Serving 675 calories, 37g fat (of which 13g saturates), 44g carbohydrate, 0.5g salt • Easy

2 lamb fillets, about 400g (14oz) each
5 tbsp olive oil
1 aubergine, cut into 1cm (½in) dice
1 tsp ground cumin
½ tsp ground cinnamon
225g (8oz) quick-cook couscous

1 large fresh red chilli, seeded and finely chopped (see Cook's Tips, page 38)
3 tbsp freshly chopped mint
75g (3oz) raisins, soaked in hot water and drained
salt and ground black pepper
Greek yogurt to serve

1. Trim the lamb fillets, rub in 1 tbsp oil and season well with salt and pepper. Heat a heavy-based non-stick pan, add the lamb and fry for 15 minutes, turning regularly. Remove from the pan and leave to rest for 5 minutes (see Cook's Tip).

2. Meanwhile, toss the aubergine in the cumin and cinnamon, then fry in 2 tbsp oil for 10 minutes or until softened. Prepare the couscous according to the pack instructions, then fluff the grains using a fork. Add the aubergine, chilli, 2 tbsp mint, the raisins and the remaining oil to the couscous. Season well with salt and pepper.

3. To serve, slice the lamb and place on top of the couscous. Drizzle with Greek yogurt, sprinkle with the remaining chopped mint and serve immediately.

COOK'S TIP
Leaving the lamb to rest for 5 minutes allows the juices to set and they won't run out.

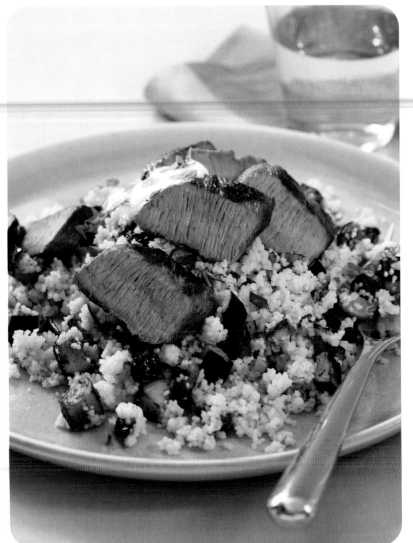

Lamb with Tapenade

Preparation Time 5 minutes, plus marinating • Cooking Time 8–10 minutes • Serves 4 • Per Serving 579 calories, 34g fat (of which 15g saturates), 0g carbohydrate, 0.4g salt • Easy

6 tbsp olive oil

4 tbsp tapenade (see Cook's Tips, page 72)

2 tbsp Pernod or Ricard

2 garlic cloves, crushed

8 loin lamb chops, about 125g (4oz) each

ground black pepper

TO SERVE

grilled sliced fennel and courgettes

4 lemon halves

1. Mix the oil with the tapenade, Pernod or Ricard and the garlic, then rub into the lamb chops and season with black pepper. Leave to marinate for at least 30 minutes or overnight.

2. Preheat the barbecue or griddle. Cook the chops for 4–5 minutes on each side. Serve with lightly grilled fennel and courgette slices, and lemon halves to squeeze over them

COOK'S TIP

The marinade is ideal for other cuts of lamb, such as steaks or fillets, or spread it over a boned shoulder or leg.

Steak with Onions & Tagliatelle

Preparation Time 10 minutes • Cooking Time 20 minutes • Serves 4 • Per Serving 557 calories,
26g fat (of which 16g saturates), 51g carbohydrate, 0.2g salt • Easy

225g (8oz) tagliatelle
2 × 200g (7oz) sirloin steaks
2 red onions, thinly sliced
200g (7oz) low-fat crème fraîche
2 tbsp freshly chopped flat-leafed
    parsley
salt and ground black pepper

1. Cook the pasta in a large pan of boiling water according to the pack instructions; do not overcook – it should be al dente. Drain well.

2. Meanwhile, season the steaks on both sides with salt and pepper. Heat a non-stick frying pan until really hot and fry the steaks for 2–3 minutes on each side until brown but still pink inside. Remove from the pan and set aside.

3. Add the onions to the pan and stir-fry for 8–10 minutes until softened and golden. Add a little water if they're sticking. Season, reduce the heat and stir in the crème fraîche.

4. Cut the fat off the steaks and discard, then cut the meat into thin strips. Add to the pan and cook briskly for 1–2 minutes, then stir in the pasta. Add the parsley, toss again and serve immediately.

Beef Stroganoff

Preparation Time 10 minutes • Cooking Time about 20 minutes • Serves 4 • Per Serving 750 calories, 60g fat (of which 35g saturates), 3g carbohydrate, 0.5g salt • Easy

700g (1½lb) rump or fillet steak, trimmed
50g (2oz) unsalted butter or 4 tbsp olive oil
1 onion, thinly sliced
225g (8oz) brown-cap mushrooms, sliced
3 tbsp brandy
1 tsp French mustard
200ml (7fl oz) crème fraîche
100ml (3½fl oz) double cream
3 tbsp freshly chopped flat-leafed parsley
salt and ground black pepper
rice or noodles to serve

1. Cut the steak into strips about 5mm (¼in) wide and 5cm (2in) long.

2. Heat half the butter or oil in a large heavy frying pan over a medium heat. Add the onion and cook gently for 10 minutes or until soft and golden. Remove with a slotted spoon and put to one side. Add the mushrooms to the pan and cook, stirring, for 2–3 minutes until golden brown; remove and put to one side.

3. Increase the heat and add the remaining butter or oil to the pan. Quickly fry the meat, in two or three batches, for 2–3 minutes, stirring constantly to ensure even browning. Remove from the pan. Add the brandy to the pan and allow it to bubble to reduce.

4. Put all the meat, onion and mushrooms back in the pan. Reduce the heat and stir in the mustard, crème fraîche and cream. Heat through, stir in most of the parsley and season with salt and pepper. Serve with rice or noodles, with the remaining parsley scattered over the top.

Sesame Beef

Preparation Time 10 minutes • Cooking Time 10 minutes • Serves 4 • Per Serving 207 calories,
10g fat (of which 3g saturates), 4g carbohydrate, 2g salt • Easy

2 tbsp soy sauce

2 tbsp Worcestershire sauce

2 tsp tomato purée

juice of ½ lemon

1 tbsp sesame seeds

1 garlic clove, crushed

400g (14oz) rump steak, sliced

1 tbsp vegetable oil

3 small pak choi, chopped

1 bunch of spring onions, sliced

freshly cooked egg noodles or
    tagliatelle to serve

1. Put the soy sauce and Worcestershire sauce, tomato purée, lemon juice, sesame seeds and garlic into a bowl. Add the steak and toss to coat.

2. Heat the oil in a large wok or non-stick frying pan until hot. Add the steak and sear well. Remove from the wok and set aside.

3. Add any sauce from the bowl to the wok and heat for 1 minute. Add the pak choi, spring onions and steak and stir-fry for 5 minutes. Add freshly cooked and drained noodles, toss and serve immediately

TRY SOMETHING DIFFERENT

Use 400g (14oz) pork escalope cut into strips instead of beef. Cook for 5 minutes before removing from the pan at step 2.

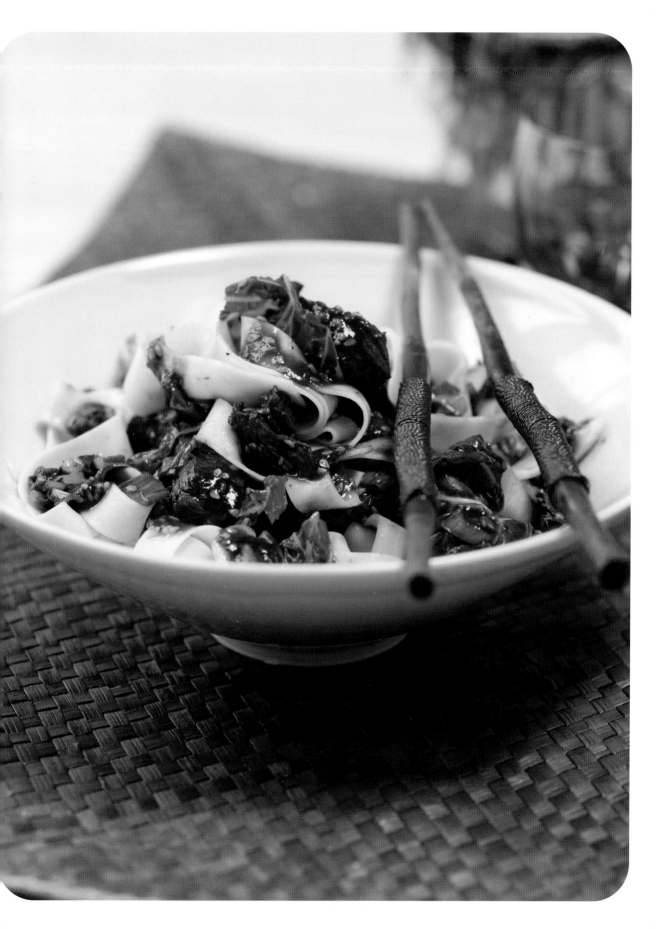

Oven-poached Cod with Herbs

Preparation Time 10 minutes • Cooking Time 10 minutes • Serves 4 • Per Serving 170 calories,
2g fat (of which trace saturates), 1g carbohydrate, 0.5g salt • Easy

10 spring onions, sliced
2 garlic cloves, crushed
6 tbsp shredded fresh mint
6 tbsp freshly chopped flat-leafed
   parsley
juice of ½ lemon
150ml (¼ pint) fish, chicken or
   vegetable stock
4 cod fillets, about 200g (7oz) each
salt and ground black pepper
lemon wedges to garnish
mashed potatoes to serve

1. Preheat the oven to 230°C (210°C fan oven) mark 8. Combine the spring onions (putting some of the green part to one side), garlic, mint, parsley, lemon juice and stock in an ovenproof dish that can hold the cod in a single layer.

2. Put the cod on the herb and garlic mixture and turn to moisten. Season with salt and pepper, then roast for 8–10 minutes.

3. Sprinkle with the reserved spring onion, garnish with lemon wedges and serve with mashed potatoes.

TRY SOMETHING DIFFERENT
There are lots of alternatives to cod: try sea bass, gurnard or pollack.

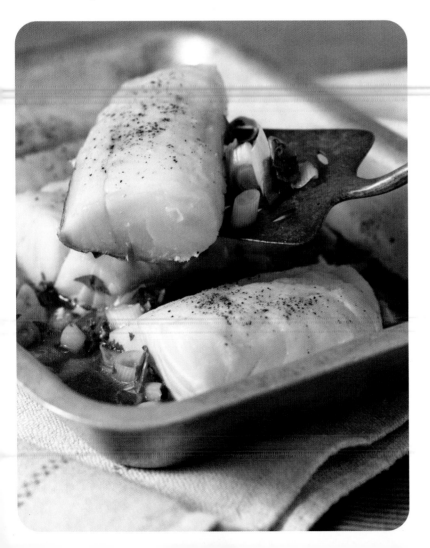

Roasted Cod with Fennel

Preparation Time 3 minutes • Cooking Time 20 minutes • Serves 4 • Per Serving 306 calories, 14g fat (of which 7g saturates), 9g carbohydrate, 0.4g salt • Easy

50g (2oz) butter
1 tbsp olive oil
2 red onions, finely sliced
2 small or 1 large fennel bulb, finely sliced
2 tbsp chopped dill, plus extra to garnish

150ml (¼ pint) dry white wine
4 × 150g (5oz) pieces cod
salt and ground black pepper
new potatoes and green beans to serve

1. Preheat the oven to 200°C (180°C fan oven) mark 6. Heat the butter and oil in a flameproof casserole dish over a medium heat. When sizzling, add the onions and fennel, then cover and cook, stirring occasionally, for 7 minutes or until soft and translucent.

2. Add the dill and wine and bring quickly to the boil. Put the fish on top of the fennel mixture and season with salt and pepper. Put the casserole dish into the oven and cook for 10 minutes, basting the fish occasionally with the juices.

3. Sprinkle with plenty of extra dill and serve immediately with new potatoes and green beans.

TRY SOMETHING DIFFERENT
• *Use haddock, coley or whiting instead of the cod.*
• *Stir 1 tbsp capers in with the dill and wine.*

Poached Thai Salmon

Preparation Time 10 minutes • Cooking Time 15 minutes • Serves 4 • Per Serving 484 calories, 19g fat (of which 3g saturates), 42g carbohydrate, 1.8g salt • Easy

200g (7oz) Thai jasmine rice

1 tbsp sesame oil

1 red chilli, seeded and finely chopped (see Cook's Tips, page 38)

5cm (2in) piece fresh root ginger, peeled and finely chopped

1 garlic clove, crushed

1–2 tbsp miso paste (see Cook's Tips)

2 tsp Thai fish sauce (see Cook's Tips)

4 skinless salmon fillets, about 150g (5oz) each

150g (5oz) fresh shiitake mushrooms, sliced

250g (9oz) pak choi, roughly chopped

100g (3½oz) baby leaf spinach

1 lime, quartered

COOK'S TIPS

• *Miso (fermented barley and soya beans) contains beneficial live enzymes that can be destroyed by boiling. Miso is best added as a flavouring at the end of cooking. It's available from Asian shops, health-food shops and larger supermarkets.*

• *Thai fish sauce is widely used in Southeast Asian cooking and is made from fermented anchovies. It adds a salty flavour to food and is called 'nam pla' in Thailand.*

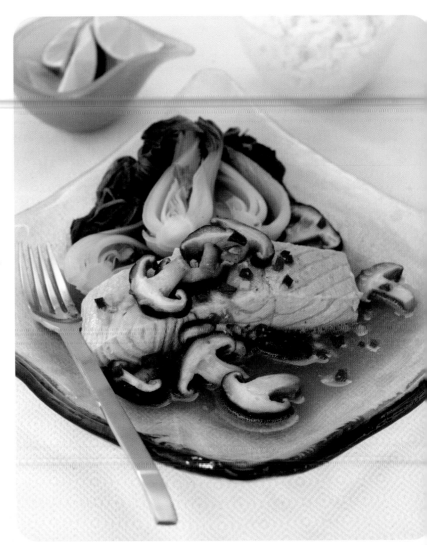

1. Put the rice into a small pan with 400ml (14fl oz) boiling water. Cover and bring to the boil, then reduce the heat to low and cook according to the pack instructions.

2. Heat the oil in a large shallow pan or wok, add the chilli, ginger and garlic and cook for 1–2 minutes. Add the miso paste and fish sauce, then pour in 500ml (18fl oz) hot water. Add the salmon and mushrooms, then cover and simmer for 7–8 minutes until fish is just cooked.

3. Steam the pak choi and spinach over boiling water for 4–5 minutes. Serve the salmon with the sauce, rice and vegetables, and lime wedges to squeeze over it.

Salmon Laksa Curry

Preparation Time 10 minutes • Cooking Time about 20 minutes • Serves 4 • Per Serving 570 calories, 22g fat (of which 3g saturates), 55g carbohydrate, 1.9g salt • Easy

1 tbsp olive oil
1 onion, thinly sliced
3 tbsp laksa paste (see Cook's Tip)
200ml (7fl oz) coconut milk
900ml (1½ pints) hot vegetable
   stock
200g (7oz) baby sweetcorn, halved
   lengthways
600g (1lb 5oz) piece skinless
   salmon fillet, cut into 1cm (½in)
   slices
225g (8oz) baby leaf spinach
250g (9oz) medium rice noodles
salt and ground black pepper

TO GARNISH
2 spring onions, sliced diagonally
2 tbsp freshly chopped coriander
1 lime, cut into wedges

1. Heat the oil in a wok or large frying pan, then add the onion and fry over a medium heat for 10 minutes, stirring, until golden. Add the laksa paste and cook for 2 minutes.

2. Add the coconut milk, hot stock and sweetcorn and season with salt and pepper. Bring to the boil, then reduce the heat and simmer for 5 minutes.

3. Add the salmon slices and spinach, stirring to immerse them in the liquid. Cook for 4 minutes or until the fish is opaque all the way through.

4. Meanwhile, put the noodles into a large heatproof bowl, pour boiling water over to cover and soak for 30 seconds. Drain well, then stir them into the curry. Pour the curry into four warmed bowls and garnish with the spring onions and coriander. Serve immediately with lime wedges.

COOK'S TIP
Laksa paste is a hot and spicy paste; you could use Thai curry paste instead.

TRY SOMETHING DIFFERENT
Instead of the medium rice noodles try using rice vermicelli, or leave out the noodles and serve with basmati rice.

Kerala Fish Curry

Preparation Time 10 minutes • Cooking Time about 20 minutes • Serves 4 • Per Serving 189 calories,
9g fat (of which 1g saturates), 5g carbohydrate, 0.5g salt • A Little Effort

4 skinless sole or plaice fillets,
   about 125g (4oz) each
2 tbsp light olive oil
1 onion, thinly sliced
1 large garlic clove, crushed
1 green chilli, slit lengthways, seeds
   in (see Cook's Tips, page 38)
2.5cm (1in) piece fresh root ginger,
   peeled and grated
1 tsp ground turmeric
1 tbsp garam masala, or about
   12 curry leaves (see Cook's Tips)

200ml (7fl oz) coconut milk
1 tbsp freshly squeezed lime juice,
   white wine vinegar or tamarind
   paste (see Cook's Tips)
salt and ground black pepper

TO SERVE
basmati rice
fresh banana leaves cut into strips
   (optional, see Cook's Tips)
1 lime, cut into wedges

1. Roll up the fish fillets from head to tail and put to one side.

2. Heat the oil in a deep frying pan over a medium heat. Stir in the onion, garlic, chilli and ginger and stir-fry for 5–7 minutes until the onion is soft. Add the turmeric and garam masala (or curry leaves, if using) and fry for a further 1–2 minutes until aromatic.

3. Pour the coconut milk into the pan along with 200ml (7fl oz) water and bring to the boil. Reduce the heat and simmer very gently, uncovered, for 7–10 minutes until slightly thickened. The sauce should be the consistency of single cream. Stir in the lime juice, vinegar or tamarind. Check the seasoning and adjust if necessary.

4. When you're ready to serve, carefully lower the rolls of fish into the hot sauce to prevent splashing and simmer very gently for 1–2 minutes until just cooked. Serve with basmati rice, in bowls lined with banana leaves if you like, with a wedge of lime to squeeze over it.

GET AHEAD
To prepare ahead *Make the sauce up to 4 hours ahead.*
To use *Gently reheat to simmering point before you add the fish.*

COOK'S TIPS
• *Buy curry leaves and banana leaves from Asian shops.*
• *Tamarind paste has a very sharp, sour flavour and is widely used in Asian and Southeast Asian cooking.*

Salmon with a Spicy Yogurt Crust

Preparation Time 10 minutes • Cooking Time 10 minutes • Serves 4 • Per Serving 250 calories,
14g fat (of which 3g saturates), 3g carbohydrate, 0.2g salt • Easy

3 tbsp freshly chopped coriander

1 garlic clove, crushed

**2.5cm (1in) piece fresh root ginger,
peeled and grated**

**½ tsp each ground cumin and
coriander**

¼ tsp cayenne pepper

150g (5oz) natural yogurt

4 × 125g (4oz) salmon fillets

salt

**lime wedges and herb salad to
serve**

1. Preheat the grill. Mix together the chopped coriander, garlic, ginger, ground cumin and coriander, the cayenne, yogurt and a pinch of salt. Add the salmon and turn to coat.

2. Grill the fish for 7–10 minutes or until cooked through. Serve with lime wedges to squeeze over the fish and a herb salad.

**TRY SOMETHING
DIFFERENT**

*Use another fish instead of salmon:
try trout or plump mackerel fillets.*

Warm Spiced Salmon Niçoise

Preparation Time 15 minutes • Cooking Time 15 minutes • Serves 4 • Per Serving 480 calories, 28g fat (of which 6g saturates), 18g carbohydrate, 0.6g salt • Easy

350g (12oz) new potatoes, thickly sliced
175g (6oz) fine green beans, halved
175g (6oz) cherry tomatoes, halved
1 small red onion, cut into thin wedges
4 × 150–175g (5–6oz) salmon fillets, skinned

15g (½oz) butter, melted
1 tbsp coriander seeds, crushed
½ tsp dried crushed chillies
4 tbsp Caesar Dressing (see Cook's Tip)
flaked sea salt and ground black pepper
fresh chives to garnish

1. Cook the potatoes in lightly salted boiling water for 8–10 minutes until just tender, adding the beans for the last 2 minutes. Drain well, then transfer to a bowl with ---the tomatoes and onion wedges. Meanwhile, preheat the grill.

2. Cut each salmon fillet into three strips. Place the strips in four piles on a baking sheet and brush each pile with the melted butter. Mix the crushed coriander seeds with the chillies and a little sea salt and sprinkle evenly over the salmon. Place under the hot grill for 4–5 minutes until just cooked through.

3. Add 1 tbsp water to the dressing to thin it slightly (it should be the consistency of single cream). Spoon three-quarters of the dressing over the vegetables and toss to coat. Season well.

4. Divide the vegetables among four plates, top with the salmon and drizzle the remaining dressing around the edge of the salad. Garnish with chives and serve.

COOK'S TIP

Caesar Dressing

Put 1 egg, 1 garlic clove, juice of ½ lemon, 2 tsp Dijon mustard and 1 tsp balsamic vinegar into a food processor and whiz until smooth, then, with the motor running, gradually add 150ml (¼ pint) sunflower oil and whiz until smooth. Season with salt and pepper, cover and chill. It will keep for up to three days.

Scallops with Ginger

Preparation Time 15 minutes • Cooking Time 3 minutes • Serves 4 • Per Serving 197 calories,
7g fat (of which 1g saturates), 6g carbohydrate, 2g salt • Easy

2 tbsp vegetable oil
500g (1lb 2oz) shelled large scallops,
    cut into 5mm (¼in) slices
4 celery sticks, sliced diagonally
1 bunch of spring onions, sliced
    diagonally
25g (1oz) piece fresh root ginger,
    peeled and shredded

2 large garlic cloves, sliced
¼ tsp chilli powder
2 tbsp lemon juice
2 tbsp light soy sauce
3 tbsp freshly chopped coriander
salt and ground black pepper
rice to serve

1. Heat the oil in a wok or large frying pan. Add the scallops, celery, spring onions, ginger, garlic and chilli powder and stir-fry over a high heat for 2 minutes or until the vegetables are just tender.

2. Pour in the lemon juice and soy sauce, allow to bubble up, then stir in about 2 tbsp chopped coriander and season with salt and pepper. Sprinkle with the remaining coriander and serve with rice.

Peppered Tuna with Olive & Herb Salsa

Preparation Time 15 minutes • Cooking Time 8–12 minutes • Serves 4 • Per Serving 398 calories, 32g fat (of which 12g saturates), 1g carbohydrate, 1.9g salt • Easy

1 tsp olive oil

zest and juice of 1 lime, plus lime wedges to serve

1 tbsp cracked mixed peppercorns

4 × 150g (5oz) tuna steaks

grilled tomatoes to serve

FOR THE OLIVE & HERB SALSA

1 tbsp extra virgin olive oil

1 tbsp each pitted black and green olives, roughly chopped

zest and juice of ½ lemon

2 tbsp freshly chopped parsley

1 tbsp freshly chopped coriander

1 tbsp capers, roughly chopped

salt and ground black pepper

1. Put the olive oil into a large shallow bowl, add the lime zest and juice and peppercorns and stir to mix. Add the tuna and turn to coat in the oil.

2. Heat a non-stick griddle pan until hot. Cook the tuna steaks, two at a time, for 2–3 minutes on each side.

3. Meanwhile, put all the ingredients for the salsa into a bowl and stir to combine. Season to taste and mix well. Serve the tuna with the salsa and grilled tomatoes, and lime wedges to squeeze over it.

TRY SOMETHING DIFFERENT
Use swordfish instead of tuna.

Plaice with Herb & Polenta Crust

Preparation Time 15 minutes • Cooking Time 4–6 minutes • Serves 2 • Per Serving 376 calories,
17g fat (of which 3g saturates), 19g carbohydrate, 0.6g salt • Easy

1 tsp finely chopped rosemary or
   1 tsp finely snipped chives
1 tsp finely chopped thyme
2 garlic cloves, very finely chopped
50g (2oz) polenta
finely grated zest and juice of
   2 small lemons

2 plaice fillets, about 175g (6oz)
   each, skinned
1 large egg
2 tbsp olive oil
salt and ground black pepper
roasted tomatoes, green beans and
   lemon wedges to serve

1. Combine the herbs, garlic and polenta on a flat plate. Add the lemon zest, salt and pepper and mix well. Wipe the plaice fillets with kitchen paper.

2. Beat the egg in a shallow dish, dip the fish fillets into the egg and coat them with the polenta mixture, pressing it on well

3. Heat the oil in a very large frying pan over a high heat. When hot, add the fish, turn the heat down to medium and cook for 2–3 minutes on each side, depending on the thickness of the fillets. Drain on kitchen paper. Serve with lemon juice poured over them, with roasted tomatoes, green beans and extra lemon wedges.

Saffron Paella

Preparation Time 5 minutes • Cooking Time 20 minutes • Serves 6 • Per Serving 609 calories, 22g fat (of which 6g saturates), 59g carbohydrate, 1.5g salt • Easy

½ tsp saffron threads

900ml–1.1 litres (1½–2 pints) hot chicken stock

5 tbsp olive oil

2 × 70g packs sliced chorizo sausage

6 boneless, skinless chicken thighs, each cut into three pieces

1 large onion, chopped

4 large garlic cloves, crushed

1 tsp paprika

2 red peppers, seeded and sliced

400g can chopped tomatoes in tomato juice

350g (12oz) long-grain rice

200ml (7fl oz) dry sherry

500g pack ready-cooked mussels

400g (14oz) cooked tiger prawns, drained

juice of ½ lemon

salt and ground black pepper

fresh flat-leafed parsley sprigs to garnish (optional)

lemon wedges to serve

1. Add the saffron to the hot stock and leave to infuse for 30 minutes. Meanwhile, heat half the oil in a large heavy-based frying pan. Add half the chorizo and fry for 3–4 minutes until crisp. Remove with a slotted spoon and drain on kitchen paper. Repeat with the remaining chorizo, then put to one side.

2. Heat 1 tbsp oil in the pan, add half the chicken and cook for 3–5 minutes until pale golden brown. Remove from the pan and put to one side. Cook the remaining chicken and put to one side.

3. Reduce the heat slightly, heat the remaining oil and add the onion. Cook for 5 minutes or until soft. Add the garlic and paprika and cook for 1 minute. Put the chicken back into the pan, then add the peppers and the tomatoes.

4. Stir the rice into the pan, then add one-third of the stock and bring to the boil. Season with salt and pepper, reduce the heat and simmer, uncovered, stirring continuously until most of the liquid has been absorbed.

5. Add the remaining stock, a little at a time, allowing the liquid to become absorbed after each addition (this should take about 25 minutes). Add the sherry and cook for a further 2 minutes.

6. Add the mussels and their juices to the pan with the prawns, lemon juice and reserved chorizo. Cook for 5 minutes to heat through. Adjust the seasoning and garnish with the parsley, if you like, and serve with lemon wedges.

Tuna with Coriander Rice

Preparation Time 10 minutes • Cooking Time about 5 minutes • Serves 4 • Per Serving 609 calories,
15g fat (of which 4g saturates), 51g carbohydrate, 0.6g salt • Easy

250g (9oz) basmati rice
8 × 125g (4oz) tuna steaks
5cm (2in) piece fresh root ginger,
**   peeled and grated**
1 tbsp olive oil
100ml (3½fl oz) orange juice
300g (11oz) pak choi, roughly
**   chopped**
a small handful of freshly chopped
**   coriander**
ground black pepper
lime wedges to garnish

1. Cook the rice according to the pack instructions.

2. Meanwhile, put the tuna steaks in a shallow dish. Add the ginger, oil and orange juice and season well with pepper. Turn the tuna over to coat.

3. Heat a non-stick frying pan until really hot. Add four tuna steaks and half the marinade and cook for 1–2 minutes on each side until just cooked. Repeat with the remaining tuna and marinade. Remove the fish from the pan and keep warm.

4. Add the pak choi to the frying pan and cook for 1–2 minutes until wilted. When the rice is cooked, drain and stir the coriander through it. Serve the tuna with the pak choi, rice and pan juices and garnish with lime wedges.

COOK'S TIP
Basmati rice should be washed before cooking to remove excess starch and to give really light, fluffy results.

Special Prawn Fried Rice

Preparation Time 5 minutes • Cooking Time 10–13 minutes • Serves 4 • Per Serving 412 calories, 18g fat (of which 3g saturates), 46g carbohydrate, 1.9g salt • Easy

2 × 250g packs of microwavable rice (see Cook's Tips)
1 tbsp sesame oil
6 tbsp nasi goreng paste (see Cook's Tips)
200g (7oz) green cabbage, shredded

250g (9oz) cooked and peeled large prawns
2 tbsp light soy sauce
1 tbsp sunflower oil
2 medium eggs, beaten
2 spring onions, thinly sliced
1 lime, cut into wedges, to serve

1. Cook the rice according to the pack instructions.

2. Heat the sesame oil in a wok and fry the nasi goreng paste for 1–2 minutes. Add the cabbage and stir-fry for 2–3 minutes. Add the prawns and stir briefly, then add the rice and soy sauce and cook for a further 5 minutes, stirring occasionally.

3. To make the omelette, heat the sunflower oil in a non-stick frying pan (about 25.5cm/10in in diameter) and add the eggs. Swirl around to cover the base of the pan in a thin layer and cook for 2–3 minutes until set.

4. Roll up the omelette and cut it into strips. Serve the rice scattered with the omelette and spring onions and pass round the lime wedges to squeeze over it.

COOK'S TIPS
● *If you can't find microwavable rice, use 200g (7oz) long-grain rice, cooked according to the pack instructions – but do not overcook. Rinse in cold water and drain well before you begin the recipe.*
● *Nasi goreng is a spicy Indonesian dish traditionally eaten for breakfast. Nasi goreng paste can be bought at most large supermarkets and Asian food shops.*

Thai Noodles with Prawns

Preparation Time 10 minutes • Cooking Time 5 minutes • Serves 4 • Per Serving 343 calories,
11g fat (of which 2g saturates), 40g carbohydrate, 1g salt • Easy

4–6 tsp Thai red curry paste
175g (6oz) medium egg noodles
(wholewheat if possible)
2 small red onions, chopped
1 lemongrass stalk, trimmed and
sliced
1 fresh red bird's-eye chilli, seeded
and finely chopped (see Cook's
Tips, page 38)

300ml (½ pint) reduced-fat coconut
milk
400g (14oz) raw tiger prawns,
peeled and deveined (see Cook's
Tip, page 139)
4 tbsp freshly chopped coriander,
plus extra freshly torn coriander
to garnish
salt and ground black pepper

1. Pour 2 litres (3½ pints) water into a large pan and bring to the boil. Add the curry paste, noodles, onions, lemongrass, chilli and coconut milk and bring back to the boil.

2. Add the prawns and chopped coriander, reduce the heat and simmer for 2–3 minutes until the prawns turn pink. Season with salt and pepper.

3. To serve, divide the noodles among four large bowls and sprinkle with the torn coriander.

Thai Green Shellfish Curry

Preparation Time 10 minutes • Cooking Time 10–15 minutes • Serves 6 • Per Serving 156 calories, 5g fat (of which 1g saturates), 6g carbohydrate, 0.8g salt • Easy

1 tbsp vegetable oil

1 lemongrass stalk, trimmed and chopped

2 small red chillies, seeded and chopped (see Cook's Tips, page 38)

a handful of fresh coriander leaves, chopped, plus extra to serve

2 kaffir lime leaves, chopped

1–2 tbsp Thai green curry paste

400ml can coconut milk

450ml (¾ pint) vegetable stock

375g (13oz) queen scallops with corals

250g (9oz) raw tiger prawns, peeled and deveined (see Cook's Tip, page 139), with tails intact

salt and ground black pepper

jasmine rice to serve

1. Heat the oil in a wok or large frying pan. Add the lemongrass, chillies, coriander and lime leaves and stir-fry for 30 seconds. Add the curry paste and fry for 1 minute.

2. Add the coconut milk and stock and bring to the boil, then reduce the heat and simmer for 5–10 minutes until slightly reduced. Season well with salt and pepper.

3. Add the scallops and tiger prawns and bring to the boil, then reduce the heat and simmer gently for 2–3 minutes until cooked.

4. Divide the rice among six bowls and spoon the curry on top. Sprinkle with coriander and serve immediately.

TRY SOMETHING DIFFERENT

Use cleaned squid or mussels instead of scallops and prawns.

VEGGIES

Aubergine, Feta & Tomato Stacks

Preparation Time 10 minutes • Cooking Time 12 minutes • Serves 4 • Per Serving 138 calories,
11g fat (of which 5g saturates), 4g carbohydrate, 1.2g salt • Vegetarian • Easy

200g (7oz) vegetarian feta cheese,
    crumbled
2 tbsp olive oil, plus extra to brush
1 garlic clove, crushed, plus 1
    garlic clove for rubbing
2 plump aubergines, cut into 1cm
    (½in) thick slices
a handful of fresh basil leaves, torn
3 large vine-ripened tomatoes,
    each sliced into four
salt and ground black pepper
rocket and toasted ciabatta to serve

1. Preheat the barbecue or grill.
Put the feta into a bowl, stir in the
oil and garlic, season with salt and
pepper and set aside.

2. Brush each aubergine slice with
a little oil and barbecue or grill
for about 6 minutes, turning
occasionally, or until softened and
golden. Remove from the heat.

3. Sprinkle a little of the feta
mixture on six of the aubergine
slices and put some torn basil
leaves on top, then a slice of
tomato on each. Season well.
Repeat with the feta mixture,
basil leaves, aubergine and tomato.
Finish with a third aubergine slice
and press down firmly.

4. Secure each stack with a
cocktail stick. Either use a hinged
grill rack, well oiled, or wrap the
stacks in foil and barbecue for
2–3 minutes on each side. Serve
with rocket leaves and toasted
ciabatta rubbed with a garlic
clove.

Baked Eggs

Preparation Time 10 minutes • Cooking Time 15 minutes • Serves 2 • Per Serving 238 calories, 21g fat (of which 5g saturates), 2g carbohydrate, 0.6g salt • Vegetarian • Easy

2 tbsp olive oil
125g (4oz) mushrooms, chopped
225g (8oz) fresh spinach
2 medium eggs
2 tbsp single cream
salt and ground black pepper

1. Preheat the oven to 200°C (180°C fan oven) mark 6. Heat the oil in a large frying pan, add the mushrooms and stir-fry for 30 seconds. Add the spinach and stir-fry until wilted. Season to taste, then divide the mixture between two shallow ovenproof dishes.

2. Carefully break an egg into the centre of each dish, then spoon 1 tbsp single cream over it.

3. Cook in the oven for about 12 minutes or until just set – the eggs will continue to cook a little once they're out of the oven. Grind a little more pepper over the top, if you like, and serve.

Cheese & Vegetable Bake

Preparation Time 15 minutes • Cooking Time 15 minutes • Serves 4 • Per Serving 471 calories,
13g fat (of which 7g saturates), 67g carbohydrate, 0.8g salt • Vegetarian • Easy

250g (9oz) macaroni

1 cauliflower, cut into florets

**2 leeks, trimmed and finely
chopped**

100g (3½oz) frozen peas

crusty bread to serve

FOR THE CHEESE SAUCE

15g (½oz) butter

15g (½oz) plain flour

200ml (7fl oz) skimmed milk

**75g (3oz) Parmesan, grated (see
Cook's Tips)**

2 tsp Dijon mustard

25g (1oz) wholemeal breadcrumbs

salt and ground black pepper

1. Cook the macaroni in a large
pan of boiling water for 6 minutes,
adding the cauliflower and leeks
for the last 4 minutes and the peas
for the last 2 minutes.

2. Meanwhile, make the cheese
sauce. Melt the butter in a pan
and add the flour. Cook for 1–2
minutes, then take off the heat and
gradually stir in the milk. Bring to
the boil slowly, stirring until the
sauce thickens. Stir in 50g (2oz)
Parmesan and the mustard.
Season with salt and pepper.

3. Preheat the grill to medium.
Drain the pasta and vegetables and
put back into the pan. Add the
cheese sauce and mix well. Spoon
into a large shallow 2 litre (3½ pint)
ovenproof dish and scatter the
remaining Parmesan and the
breadcrumbs over the top. Grill for
5 minutes or until golden and crisp.
Serve hot with bread.

COOK'S TIPS

Microwave Cheese Sauce
*Put the butter, flour and milk into a
large microwave-proof bowl and
whisk together. Cook in a 900W
microwave oven on full power for
4 minutes, whisking every minute,
until the sauce has thickened. Stir in
the cheese until it melts. Stir in the
mustard and season to taste.*

*Vegetarian cheeses: some
vegetarians prefer to avoid cheeses
that have been produced by the
traditional method, because this
uses animal-derived rennet. Most
supermarkets and cheese shops
now stock an excellent range of
vegetarian cheeses, produced
using vegetarian rennet, which
comes from plants, such as thistle
and mallow, that contain enzymes
capable of curdling milk.*

Chickpea & Butternut Pot

Preparation Time 10 minutes • Cooking Time 15–20 minutes • Serves 4 • Per Serving 307 calories, 14g fat (of which 2g saturates), 34g carbohydrate, 2.8g salt • Vegetarian • Easy

1 large butternut squash, peeled, seeded and chopped
2 tbsp smooth peanut butter
900ml (1½ pints) hot vegetable stock
2 tbsp olive oil
2 large onions, finely chopped
1 small red chilli, seeded and finely chopped (see Cook's Tips, page 38)
2 tsp mild curry paste (see Cook's Tip, page 72)
225g (8oz) baby sweetcorn
2 x 400g cans chickpeas, drained and rinsed
a handful of freshly chopped coriander
salt and ground black pepper

1. Put the butternut squash, peanut butter and hot stock in a large pan and simmer for 10 minutes until the squash is tender. Remove three-quarters of the squash with a slotted spoon and put to one side. Mash the remaining squash into -the liquid, then put the reserved squash back into the pan.

2. Meanwhile, heat the oil in a pan over a low heat and fry the onions, chilli, curry paste and sweetcorn until the onions are soft and caramelised, then tip the contents of the pan into the squash.

3. Add the chickpeas and coriander to the squash and stir through. Season with salt and pepper and cook for 4–5 minutes until piping hot. Serve immediately.

Mushroom Soufflé Omelette

Preparation Time 5 minutes • Cooking Time 7–10 minutes • Serves 1 • Per Serving 440 calories,
42g fat (of which 23g saturates), 2g carbohydrate, 0.6g salt • Vegetarian • Easy

**50g (2oz) small chestnut
    mushrooms, sliced**
3 tbsp crème fraîche
2 medium eggs, separated
15g (½oz) butter
5 fresh chives, roughly chopped
salt and ground black pepper

1. Heat a non-stick frying pan for 30 seconds. Add the mushrooms and cook, stirring, for 3 minutes to brown slightly, then stir in the crème fraîche and turn off the heat.

2. Lightly beat the egg yolks in a bowl, add 2 tbsp cold water and season with salt and pepper.

3. In a separate clean, grease-free bowl, whisk the egg whites until stiff but not dry, then gently fold into the egg yolks. Do not over-mix. Heat an 18cm (7in) non-stick frying pan over a medium heat. Add the butter, then the egg mixture, tilting the pan to cover the base. Cook for 3 minutes or until the underside is golden brown.

4. Meanwhile, preheat the grill. Gently reheat the mushrooms and add the chives. Put the omelette under the grill for 1 minute or until the surface is just firm and puffy. Tip the mushroom mixture on top. Run a spatula around and underneath the omelette to loosen it, then carefully fold it and turn out on to a warmed plate. Serve immediately.

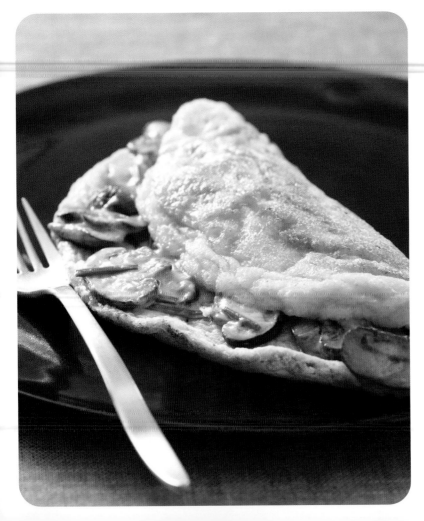

Camembert & Tomato Tarts

Preparation Time 10 minutes • Cooking Time 15–20 minutes • Serves 4 • Per Serving 253 calories,
17g fat (of which 4g saturates), 19g carbohydrate, 1.1g salt • Vegetarian • Easy

½ × 375g pack ready-rolled puff
    pastry
2 tbsp tapenade (see Cook's Tips,
    page 72)
200g (7oz) cherry tomatoes, halved
75g (3oz) Camembert, sliced (see
    Cook's Tips, page 190)

1. Preheat the oven to 220°C
(200°C fan oven) mark 7. Cut the
puff pastry into four pieces. Put
on a baking sheet and cook for
8–10 minutes until risen.

2. Press down the centre of each
tart slightly with the back of a fish
slice, then spread this area with the
tapenade. Top with the tomatoes
and sliced Camembert. Put back
into the oven for a further 7–8
minutes until golden brown.

Couscous-stuffed Mushrooms

Preparation Time 3 minutes • Cooking Time about 12 minutes • Serves 4 • Per Serving 373 calories,
25g fat (of which 10g saturates), 25g carbohydrate, 0.6g salt • Vegetarian • Easy

125g (4oz) couscous

20g pack fresh flat-leafed parsley, roughly chopped

280g jar mixed antipasti in oil, drained and oil put to one side

8 large flat portabellini mushrooms

25g (1oz) butter

25g (1oz) plain flour

300ml (½ pint) skimmed milk

75g (3oz) mature vegetarian Cheddar, grated, plus extra to sprinkle

green salad to serve

1. Preheat the oven to 220°C (200°C fan oven) mark 7. Put the couscous into a bowl with 200ml (7fl oz) boiling water, the parsley, antipasti and 1 tbsp of the reserved oil. Stir well.

2. Put the mushrooms on a non-stick baking tray and spoon a little of the couscous mixture into the centre of each. Cook in the oven while you make the sauce.

3. Whisk together the butter, flour and milk in a small pan over a high heat until the mixture comes to the boil. Reduce the heat as soon as it starts to thicken, then whisk constantly until smooth. Take the pan off the heat and stir in the cheese.

4. Spoon the sauce over the mushrooms and sprinkle with the remaining cheese. Put back into the oven for a further 7–10 minutes until golden. Serve with a green salad.

Polenta with Mixed Mushrooms

Preparation Time 10 minutes • Cooking Time 20 minutes • Serves 6 • Per Serving 383 calories, 13g fat (of which 4g saturates), 56g carbohydrate, 0.1g salt • Vegetarian • Easy

50g (2oz) butter

1.1kg (2½lb) mixed mushrooms

1 red chilli, seeded and finely chopped (see Cook's Tips, page 38)

3 garlic cloves, sliced

100g (3½oz) sun-dried tomatoes, roughly chopped

1 tsp freshly chopped thyme, plus thyme sprigs to garnish

1kg (2¼lb) ready-made polenta

3 tbsp olive oil

truffle oil (optional)

salt and ground black pepper

1. Melt half the butter in a deep-sided frying pan or wok. Add half the mushrooms and cook over a high heat until all the liquid has evaporated, then set aside. Repeat with the remaining butter and mushrooms. Add the chilli and garlic to the pan and fry for 2 minutes, then add to the mushrooms, together with the sun-dried tomatoes and thyme. Mix well and season with salt and pepper.

2. Slice the polenta into 12 pieces, about 1cm (½in) thick. Heat the oil in a non-stick frying pan. Add the polenta in batches and fry for 3–4 minutes on each side or until golden.

3. To serve, arrange two slices of polenta per person on a plate, top with the mushroom mixture and drizzle with a little truffle oil, if using. Garnish with thyme sprigs.

Spinach & Goat's Cheese Frittata

Preparation Time 10 minutes • Cooking Time 12 minutes • Serves 4 • Per Serving 281 calories,
21g fat (of which 9g saturates), 3g carbohydrate, 0.9g salt • Easy

**200g (7oz) baby leeks, trimmed and
     chopped**
4 spring onions, chopped
125g (4oz) baby leaf spinach
6 large eggs
4 tbsp milk
freshly grated nutmeg
**125g (4oz) soft goat's cheese,
     chopped**
1 tbsp olive oil
salt and ground black pepper
mixed salad leaves to serve

1. Preheat the grill to high. Blanch the leeks in a pan of lightly salted boiling water for 2 minutes. Add the spring onions and spinach just before the end of the cooking time. Drain, rinse in cold water and dry on kitchen paper.

2. Whisk together the eggs, milk and nutmeg. Season with salt and pepper. Stir the goat's cheese into the egg mixture with the leeks, spinach and spring onions.

3. Heat the oil in a non-stick frying pan. Pour in the frittata mixture and fry gently for 4–5 minutes, then finish under the hot grill for 4–5 minutes until the top is golden and just firm. Serve with mixed salad.

TRY SOMETHING DIFFERENT
Use a different cheese, such as Stilton.

Black-eye Bean Chilli

Preparation Time 10 minutes • Cooking Time 20 minutes • Serves 4 • Per Serving 245 calories,
5g fat (of which 1g saturates), 39g carbohydrate, 1.8g salt • Vegetarian • Easy

1 tbsp olive oil
1 onion, chopped
3 celery sticks, finely chopped
2 × 400g cans black-eye beans,
    drained and rinsed
2 × 400g cans chopped tomatoes
2 or 3 splashes of Tabasco sauce
3 tbsp freshly chopped coriander
4 warmed tortillas and soured
    cream to serve

1. Heat the oil in a frying pan.
Add the onion and celery and cook
for 10 minutes until softened.

2. Add the beans, tomatoes and
Tabasco to the pan. Bring to the
boil, then reduce the heat and
simmer for 10 minutes.

3. Just before serving, stir in the
coriander. Spoon the Chilli on to
the warm tortillas, roll up and serve
with soured cream.

**TRY SOMETHING
DIFFERENT**
*Replace half the black-eye beans
with red kidney beans.*

Stir-fried Beans with Cherry Tomatoes

Preparation Time 10 minutes • Cooking Time about 8 minutes • Serves 6 • Per Serving 30 calories,
2g fat (of which trace saturates), 3g carbohydrate, 0g salt • Vegetarian • Easy

350g (12oz) green beans, trimmed
2 tsp olive oil
1 large garlic clove, crushed
**150g (5oz) cherry or baby plum
   tomatoes, halved**
**2 tbsp freshly chopped flat-leafed
   parsley**
salt and ground black pepper

1. Cook the beans in lightly salted boiling water for 4–5 minutes, then drain well.

2. Heat the oil in a wok or large frying pan over a high heat. Stir-fry the beans with the garlic and tomatoes for 2–3 minutes until the beans are tender and the tomatoes are just beginning to soften without losing their shape. Season well with salt and pepper, stir in the parsley and serve.

Chickpea & Chilli Stir-fry

Preparation Time 10 minutes • Cooking Time 15–20 minutes • Serves 4 • Per Serving 258 calories,
11g fat (of which 1g saturates), 30g carbohydrate, 1g salt • Vegetarian • Easy

2 tbsp olive oil

1 tsp ground cumin

1 red onion, sliced

2 garlic cloves, finely chopped

**1 red chilli, seeded and finely
chopped (see Cook's Tips,
page 38)**

**2 × 400g cans chickpeas, drained
and rinsed**

400g (14oz) cherry tomatoes

125g (4oz) baby spinach leaves

brown rice or pasta to serve

1. Heat the oil in a wok or large frying pan. Add the cumin and fry for 1–2 minutes. Add the onion and stir-fry for 5–7 minutes.

2. Add the garlic and chilli and stir-fry for 2 minutes.

3. Add the chickpeas to the wok with the tomatoes. Reduce the heat and simmer until the chickpeas are hot. Season with salt and pepper. Add the spinach and cook for 1–2 minutes until the leaves have wilted. Serve with brown rice or pasta.

Summer Vegetable Stir-fry

Preparation Time 15 minutes • Cooking Time 7–8 minutes • Serves 4 • Per Serving 78 calories, 4g fat (of which 1g saturates), 7g carbohydrate, trace salt • Vegetarian • Easy

125g (4oz) baby carrots, scrubbed
and trimmed
1 tbsp sesame seeds
2 tbsp sunflower oil
2 garlic cloves, roughly chopped
125g (4oz) baby courgettes, halved
lengthways

1 large yellow pepper, seeded and
cut into thick strips
125g (4oz) thin asparagus spears,
trimmed
125g (4oz) cherry tomatoes, halved
2 tbsp balsamic or sherry vinegar
1 tsp sesame oil
salt and ground black pepper

1. Blanch the carrots in lightly salted boiling water for 2 minutes, then drain and pat dry.

2. Toast the sesame seeds in a hot dry wok or large frying pan over a medium heat, stirring until they turn golden. Tip on to a plate.

3. Return the wok or frying pan to the heat, add the sunflower oil and heat until it is smoking. Add the garlic to the oil and stir-fry for 20 seconds. Add the carrots, courgettes, yellow pepper and asparagus and stir-fry over a high heat for 1 minute.

4. Add the tomatoes and season to taste with salt and pepper. Stir-fry for 3–4 minutes until the vegetables are just tender. Add the vinegar and sesame oil, toss well and sprinkle with the toasted sesame seeds. Serve immediately.

TRY SOMETHING DIFFERENT
Vary the vegetables, but always blanch the harder ones first. For a winter vegetable stir-fry, use cauliflower and broccoli florets, carrot sticks, 2–3 sliced spring onions and a little chopped fresh root ginger.

Sweet Chilli Tofu Stir-fry

Preparation Time 5 minutes, plus marinating • Cooking Time 12 minutes • Serves 4 • Per Serving 167 calories,
11g fat (of which 2g saturates), 5g carbohydrate, 1.6g salt • Vegetarian • Easy

200g (7oz) firm tofu
4 tbsp sweet chilli sauce
2 tbsp light soy sauce
1 tbsp sesame seeds
2 tbsp toasted sesame oil
600g (1lb 5oz) ready-prepared
  mixed stir-fry vegetables, such
  as carrots, broccoli, mangetouts
  and bean sprouts
a handful of pea shoots or young
  salad leaves to garnish
rice to serve

1. Drain the tofu, pat it dry and cut it into large cubes. Put the tofu into a shallow container and pour 1 tbsp sweet chilli sauce and 1 tbsp light soy sauce over it. Cover and marinate for 10 minutes.

2. Meanwhile, toast the sesame seeds in a hot wok or large frying pan until golden. Tip on to a plate.

3. Return the wok or frying pan to the heat and add 1 tbsp sesame oil. Add the marinated tofu and stir-fry for 5 minutes until golden. Remove and set aside.

4. Heat the remaining 1 tbsp oil in the pan, add the vegetables and stir-fry for 3–4 minutes until just tender. Stir in the cooked tofu.

5. Pour the remaining sweet chilli sauce and soy sauce into the pan, toss well and cook for a further minute until heated through. Sprinkle with the toasted sesame seeds and pea shoots or salad leaves, and serve immediately, with rice.

Thai Vegetable Curry

Preparation Time 10 minutes • Cooking Time 15 minutes • Serves 4 • Per Serving 200 calories,
10g fat (of which 2g saturates), 19g carbohydrate, 0.7g salt • Vegetarian • Easy

**2–3 tbsp red Thai curry paste (see
Cook's Tip)**

**2.5cm (1in) piece fresh root ginger,
peeled and finely chopped**

50g (2oz) cashew nuts

400ml can coconut milk

3 carrots, cut into thin batons

1 broccoli head, cut into florets

**20g (¾oz) fresh coriander, roughly
chopped**

zest and juice of 1 lime

2 large handfuls of spinach leaves

basmati rice to serve

1. Put the curry paste into a large pan, add the ginger and cashew nuts and stir-fry over a medium heat for 2–3 minutes.

2. Add the coconut milk, cover and bring to the boil. Stir the carrots into the pan, then reduce the heat and simmer for 5 minutes. Add the broccoli florets and simmer for a further 5 minutes until tender.

3. Stir the coriander and lime zest into the pan with the spinach. Squeeze the lime juice over and serve with basmati rice.

TRY SOMETHING DIFFERENT
Replace carrots and/or broccoli with alternative vegetables – try baby sweetcorn, sugarsnap peas or mangetouts and simmer for only 5 minutes until tender.

COOK'S TIP
Check the ingredients in the Thai curry paste: some contain shrimp and are therefore not suitable for vegetarians.

Spiced Egg Pilau

Preparation Time 5 minutes • Cooking Time 15 minutes • Serves 4 • Per Serving 331 calories,
9g fat (of which 12g saturates), 50g carbohydrate, 0.6g salt • Vegetarian • Easy

200g (7oz) basmati or wild rice
150g (5oz) frozen peas
4 medium eggs
200ml (7fl oz) coconut cream
1 tsp mild curry paste (see Cook's
Tip, page 67)
1 tbsp sweet chilli sauce
1 tbsp smooth peanut butter
1 large bunch of fresh coriander,
roughly chopped
mini poppadums and mango
chutney to serve

1. Put the rice into a pan with
450ml (¾ pint) boiling water over
a low heat and cook for 15 minutes
or until just tender. Add the peas
for the last 5 minutes of cooking
time.

2. Meanwhile, put the eggs into a
large pan of boiling water, then
reduce the heat and simmer for
6 minutes, then drain and shell.

3. Put the coconut cream, curry
paste, chilli sauce and peanut
butter into a small pan and whisk
together. Heat the sauce gently,
stirring, without allowing it to boil.

4. Drain the rice and stir in the
chopped coriander and 2 tbsp of
the sauce.

5. Divide the rice among four
bowls. Cut the eggs into halves
and serve on the rice, spooning
the remaining coconut sauce over
the top. Serve with poppadums and
chutney.

Asparagus & Mangetouts with Lemon Sauce

Preparation Time 5–10 minutes • Cooking Time 10 minutes • Serves 4 • Per Serving 114 calories, 6g fat (of which 1g saturates), 10g carbohydrate, trace salt • Vegetarian • Easy

225g (8oz) asparagus spears,
   trimmed and cut diagonally into
   three pieces
1 tbsp sesame seeds
1 tbsp vegetable oil
1 tsp sesame oil
225g (8oz) mangetouts
1 garlic clove, crushed

2 tbsp dry sherry
1 tbsp caster sugar
2 tsp light soy sauce
grated zest and juice of 1 lemon
1 tsp cornflour
salt
strips of lemon zest to garnish

1. Cook the asparagus in a pan of lightly salted boiling water for about 5 minutes until just tender. Drain well.

2. Meanwhile, toast the sesame seeds in a hot wok or large frying pan until golden. Tip on to a plate.

3. Return the wok or frying pan to the heat and add the vegetable and sesame oils. Add the mangetouts, garlic and asparagus and stir-fry for 2 minutes.

4. Put the sherry, sugar, soy sauce, lemon zest and juice, cornflour and 5 tbsp water into a bowl and mix well.

5. Pour the mixture into the pan and cook, stirring, until the sauce thickens and coats the vegetables. Sprinkle with the toasted sesame seeds, garnish with lemon zest and serve immediately.

Chickpeas with Spinach

Preparation Time 10 minutes • Cooking Time 12–15 minutes • Serves 6 • Per Serving 204 calories,
10g fat (of which 1g saturates), 21g carbohydrate, 0.8g salt • Vegetarian • Easy

3 tbsp olive oil

2.5cm (1in) piece fresh root ginger,
   peeled and finely chopped

3 garlic cloves, chopped

2 tsp each ground coriander and
   paprika

1 tsp ground cumin

2 × 400g cans chickpeas, drained
   and rinsed

4 tomatoes, roughly chopped

a handful of coriander leaves

450g (1lb) fresh spinach

salt and ground black pepper

rice and grated carrots with lemon
   juice to serve

1. Heat the oil in a large heavy-
based pan, add the ginger, garlic
and spices and cook for 2 minutes,
stirring. Stir in the chickpeas.

2. Add the tomatoes to the pan
with the coriander leaves and
spinach and cook gently for
10 minutes. Season to taste
with salt and pepper and serve
immediately, with rice and a salad
of grated carrots tossed in a little
lemon juice.

Mixed Beans with Lemon Vinaigrette

Preparation Time 15 minutes • Serves 6 • Per Serving 285 calories, 19g fat (of which 3g saturates), 22g carbohydrate, 1g salt • Vegetarian • Easy

400g can mixed beans, drained and rinsed

400g can chickpeas, drained and rinsed

2 shallots, finely chopped

fresh mint sprigs and lemon zest to garnish

FOR THE VINAIGRETTE

2 tbsp lemon juice

2 tsp clear honey

8 tbsp extra virgin olive oil

3 tbsp freshly chopped mint

4 tbsp freshly chopped flat-leafed parsley

salt and ground black pepper

1. Put the beans and chickpeas into a bowl and add the shallots.

2. To make the vinaigrette, whisk together the lemon juice, honey and salt and pepper to taste. Gradually whisk in the oil and stir in the chopped herbs. Just before serving, pour the dressing over the bean mixture and toss well.

3. Transfer the salad to a serving dish, garnish with mint sprigs and lemon zest and serve immediately.

GET AHEAD

To prepare ahead Complete the recipe to the end of step 2 but don't add the herbs to the vinaigrette. Cover and chill for up to two days. *To use* Remove from the fridge up to 1 hour before serving, stir in the herbs and complete the recipe.

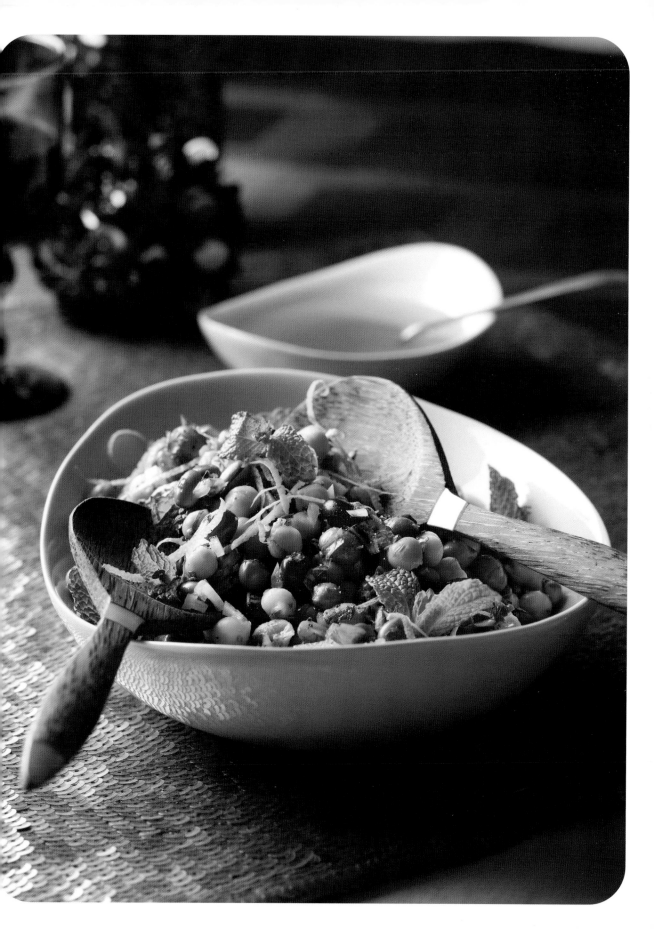

Pasta with Vegetables, Pinenuts & Pesto

Preparation Time 5 minutes • Cooking Time 15 minutes • Serves 4 • Per Serving 556 calories, 27g fat (of which 6g saturates), 60g carbohydrate, 0.5g salt • Vegetarian • Easy

300g (11oz) penne pasta
50g (2oz) pinenuts
1 tbsp olive oil
1 garlic clove, crushed
250g (9oz) closed-cup mushrooms, sliced

2 courgettes, sliced
250g (9oz) cherry tomatoes
6 tbsp fresh Pesto (see Cook's Tip, page 80)
25g (1oz) Parmesan shavings (see Cook's Tips, pages 46 and 190)

1. Cook the pasta in a large pan of lightly salted boiling water according to the pack instructions.

2. Meanwhile, gently toast the pinenuts in a dry frying pan, tossing them around until golden, then remove from the pan and set aside. Add the oil to the pan, followed by the garlic, mushrooms and courgettes. Add a splash of water to the pan, then cover and cook for 4–5 minutes.

3. Uncover the pan and add the tomatoes, then cook for a further 1–2 minutes.

4. Drain the pasta and return to the pan. Add the vegetables, pinenuts and pesto to the drained pasta. Toss well to combine and serve immediately, topped with the Parmesan shavings.

Fusilli with Chilli & Tomatoes

Preparation Time 10 minutes • Cooking Time 10–15 minutes • Serves 4 • Per Serving 479 calories,
17g fat (of which 4g saturates), 69g carbohydrate, 0.4g salt • Vegetarian • Easy

**350g (12oz) fusilli or other short
   pasta**
4 tbsp olive oil
**1 large red chilli, seeded and finely
   chopped (see Cook's Tips,
   page 38)**
1 garlic clove, crushed
500g (1lb 2oz) cherry tomatoes
2 tbsp freshly chopped basil
**50g (2oz) Parmesan shavings (see
   Cook's Tips, pages 46 and 190)**
salt and ground black pepper

1. Cook the pasta in a large pan of lightly salted boiling water according to the pack instructions. Drain.

2. Meanwhile, heat the oil in a large frying pan over a high heat. Add the chilli and garlic, and cook for 30 seconds. Add the tomato, season with salt and pepper and cook over a high heat for 3 minutes or until the skins begin to split.

3. Add the basil and drained pasta and toss together. Transfer to a serving dish, sprinkle the Parmesan shavings over the top and serve immediately.

Pasta with Goat's Cheese & Sunblush Tomatoes

Preparation Time 5 minutes • Cooking Time 10 minutes • Serves 4 • Per Serving 409 calories, 12g fat (of which 4g saturates), 64g carbohydrate, 0.4g salt • Easy

300g (11oz) conchiglie pasta

2 tbsp olive oil

1 red pepper, seeded and chopped

1 yellow pepper, seeded and chopped

½ tbsp sun-dried tomato paste

75g (3oz) sunblush tomatoes

75g (3oz) soft goat's cheese

2 tbsp freshly chopped parsley

salt and ground black pepper

1. Cook the pasta in a large pan of lightly salted boiling water according to the pack instructions until al dente.

2. Meanwhile, heat the oil in a pan and fry the red and yellow peppers for 5–7 minutes until softened and just beginning to brown. Add the tomato paste and cook for a further minute. Add a ladleful of pasta cooking water to the pan and simmer for 1–2 minutes to make a sauce.

3. Drain the pasta and return to the pan. Pour the sauce on top, then add the tomatoes, goat's cheese and parsley. Toss together until the cheese begins to melt, then season with pepper and serve.

Pea, Mint & Ricotta Pasta

Preparation Time 5 minutes • Cooking Time 10 minutes • Serves 4 • Per Serving 431 calories,
14g fat (of which 5g saturates), 63g carbohydrate, trace salt • Vegetarian • Easy

300g (11oz) farfalle pasta
200g (7oz) frozen peas
175g (6oz) ricotta cheese (see
   Cook's Tips, page 190)
3 tbsp freshly chopped mint
2 tbsp extra virgin olive oil
salt and ground black pepper

1. Cook the pasta according to
the pack instructions. Add the
frozen peas for the last 4 minutes
of cooking.

2. Drain the pasta and peas,
reserving a ladleful of pasta
cooking water, then return to the
pan. Stir in the ricotta and mint with
the pasta water. Season well, drizzle
with the oil and serve at once.

Tomato & Artichoke Pasta

Preparation Time 10 minutes • Cooking Time 10–12 minutes • Serves 4 • Per Serving 380 calories, 11g fat (of which 4g saturates), 59g carbohydrate, 1.3g salt • Vegetarian • Easy

300g (11oz) penne pasta
6 pieces sunblush tomatoes in oil
1 red onion, sliced
about 10 pieces roasted artichoke
  hearts in oil, drained and
  roughly chopped
50g (2oz) pitted black olives,
  roughly chopped
50g (2oz) pecorino cheese, grated
  (see Cook's Tips, page 190)
100g (3½oz) rocket

1. Cook the pasta in a large pan of boiling water according to the pack instructions; do not overcook – it should be al dente. Drain well.

2. Meanwhile, drain the sunblush tomatoes, reserving the oil, and roughly chop. Heat 1 tbsp oil from the tomatoes in a large frying pan, add the onion and fry for 5–6 minutes until softened and turning golden. Add the tomatoes, artichokes and olives to the pan and heat for 3–4 minutes until hot.

3. Add half the cheese and stir in. Remove from the heat and stir in the rocket and pasta. Divide the pasta among four bowls and sprinkle the remaining pecorino over the top to serve.

Pesto Gnocchi

Preparation Time 10 minutes • Cooking Time 10 minutes • Serves 4 • Per Serving 481 calories, 24g fat (of which 6g saturates), 56g carbohydrate, 0.4g salt • Vegetarian • Easy

800g (1lb 12oz) fresh gnocchi
200g (7oz) green beans, trimmed and chopped
125g (4oz) fresh Pesto (see Cook's Tip, page 80)
10 sunblush tomatoes, roughly chopped

1. Cook the gnocchi in a large pan of lightly salted boiling water according to the pack instructions or until all the gnocchi have floated to the surface. Add the beans to the water for the last 3 minutes of cooking time.

2. Drain the gnocchi and beans and put back into the pan. Add the pesto and tomatoes and toss well. Serve immediately.

PUDDINGS & DESSERTS

Quick Apple Tart

Preparation Time 10 minutes • Cooking Time 20–25 minutes • Serves 8 • Per Serving 221 calories,
12g fat (of which 0g saturates), 29g carbohydrate, 0.4g salt • Vegetarian • Easy

375g packet all-butter ready-rolled puff pastry
500g (1lb 2oz) Cox's Orange Pippin apples, cored, thinly sliced and tossed in the juice of 1 lemon
golden icing sugar to dust

1. Preheat the oven to 200°C (180°C fan oven) mark 6. Put the pastry on a 28 x 38cm (11 x 15in) baking sheet and roll lightly with a rolling pin to smooth down the pastry. Score lightly around the edge, to create a 3cm (1¼ in) border.

2. Put the apple slices on top of the pastry, within the border. Turn the edge of the pastry halfway over, so that it reaches the edge of the apples, then press down and use your fingers to crimp the edge. Dust heavily with icing sugar.

3. Bake in the oven for 20–25 minutes until the pastry is cooked and the sugar has caramelised. Serve warm, dusted with more icing sugar.

Baked Apricots with Almonds

Preparation Time 5 minutes • Cooking Time 20–25 minutes • Serves 6 • Per Serving 124 calories,
6g fat (of which 2g saturates), 16g carbohydrate, 0.1g salt • Vegetarian • Easy

12 apricots, halved and stoned
3 tbsp golden caster sugar
2 tbsp Amaretto liqueur
25g (1oz) unsalted butter
25g (1oz) flaked almonds
crème fraîche to serve

1. Preheat the oven to 200°C (180°C fan oven) mark 6. Put the apricot halves, cut side up, into an ovenproof dish. Sprinkle with the sugar, drizzle with the liqueur, then dot each apricot half with a little butter. Scatter the flaked almonds over them.

2. Bake in the oven for 20–25 minutes until the apricots are soft and the juices are syrupy. Serve warm, with crème fraîche.

TRY SOMETHING DIFFERENT
Use nectarines or peaches instead of apricots.

Ginger-glazed Pineapple

Preparation Time 10 minutes • Cooking Time 10 minutes • Serves 6 • Per Serving 88 calories, trace fat,
22g carbohydrate, 0g salt • Vegetarian • Easy

2 pineapples
2 tbsp light muscovado sugar
2 tsp ground ginger
honey and natural yogurt (optional)
to serve

1. Cut the pineapples into quarters lengthways, leaving the stalk intact. Remove the core, extract the flesh and reserve the skin. Then cut the flesh into pieces and return to the pineapple shell. Wrap the green leaves of the stalk in foil.

2. Preheat the grill. Mix the sugar with the ginger. Sprinkle each pineapple quarter with the sugar mixture. Put on foil-lined baking sheets and grill for 10 minutes until golden and caramelised. Serve with natural yogurt, if you like, and a drizzle of runny honey.

COOK'S TIP
This is the perfect dessert after a heavy or rich meal. Fresh pineapple contains an enzyme, bromelin, which digests protein very effectively and helps balance any excess acidity or alkalinity. Ginger is a well-known digestive and has many therapeutic properties.

Sticky Maple Syrup Pineapple

Preparation Time 15 minutes • Cooking Time 5 minutes • Serves 4 • Per Serving 231 calories, trace fat, 60g carbohydrate, 0.3g salt • Vegetarian • Easy

1 large pineapple
200ml (7fl oz) maple syrup

1. Peel the pineapple and cut into quarters lengthways. Cut away the central woody core from each pineapple quarter. Slice each one lengthways into four to make 16 wedges.

2. Pour the maple syrup into a large non-stick frying pan and heat for 2 minutes. Add the pineapple and fry for 3 minutes, turning once, until warmed through.

3. Divide the pineapple among four plates, drizzle the maple syrup over and around the pineapple and serve immediately.

Griddled Peaches

Preparation Time 15 minutes • Cooking Time 6–8 minutes • Serves 4 • Per Serving 94 calories,
5g fat (of which 1g saturates), 11g carbohydrate, 0g salt • Vegetarian • Easy

**4 ripe but firm peaches, halved
  and stoned**
1 tbsp maple syrup
1 tsp light olive oil
25g (1oz) pecan nuts, toasted

1. Cut the peaches into thick slices, then put into a bowl with the maple syrup and toss to coat.

2. Heat the oil in a griddle or large frying pan, add the peaches and cook for 3–4 minutes on each side until starting to char and caramelise. Sprinkle with the toasted pecan nuts and serve at once.

TRY SOMETHING DIFFERENT
Use nectarines instead of peaches, or 8 plump plums.

Peach Brûlée

Preparation Time 10 minutes • Cooking Time about 10 minutes • Serves 4 • Per Serving 137 calories,
6g fat (of which 4g saturates), 21g carbohydrate, 0.1g salt • Vegetarian • Easy

4 ripe peaches, halved and stoned
8 tsp soft cream cheese
8 tsp golden caster sugar

1. Preheat the grill until very hot.
Fill each stone cavity in the fruit
with 2 tsp cream cheese, then
sprinkle each one with 2 tsp caster
sugar.

2. Put the fruit halves on a grill pan,
and cook under the very hot grill
until the sugar has browned and
caramelised to create a brûlée
crust. Serve warm.

**TRY SOMETHING
DIFFERENT**
Use nectarines instead of peaches.

Mango Gratin with Sabayon

Preparation Time 5 minutes, plus optional resting • Cooking Time 10 minutes • Serves 6 • Per Serving 249 calories, 5g fat (of which 1g saturates), 45g carbohydrate, 0g salt • Vegetarian • A Little Effort

3 large ripe mangoes, peeled, stoned and sliced
5 medium egg yolks
6 tbsp golden caster sugar
300ml (½ pint) champagne or sparkling wine
6 tbsp dark muscovado sugar to sprinkle
crisp sweet biscuits to serve

1. Arrange the mangoes in 6 glasses. Whisk the egg yolks and sugar in a large heatproof bowl over a pan of gently simmering water until the mixture is thick and falls in soft ribbon shapes. Add the champagne or sparkling wine and continue to whisk until the mixture is thick and foamy again. Remove from the heat.

2. Spoon the sabayon over the mangoes, sprinkle with the muscovado sugar, then, if you have one, blow-torch the top to caramelise or leave for 10 minutes to go fudgey. Serve with biscuits.

Poached Plums with Port

Preparation Time 5 minutes • Cooking Time 20 minutes • Serves 4 • Per Serving 97 calories, 0g fat, 23g carbohydrate, 0g salt • Vegetarian • Easy

75g (3oz) golden caster sugar
2 tbsp port
6 large plums, halved and stoned
1 cinnamon stick
ice cream to serve (optional)

1. Put the sugar into a pan with 500ml (18fl oz) water. Heat gently until the sugar dissolves. Bring to the boil and simmer rapidly for 2 minutes without stirring.

2. Stir in the port. Add the plums to the pan with the cinnamon stick, and simmer gently for 5–10 minutes until the fruit is tender but still keeping its shape.

3. Remove the plums and put to one side, discarding the cinnamon. Simmer the syrup until it has reduced by two-thirds. Serve the plums warm or cold, drizzled with syrup and with a scoop of vanilla ice cream alongside, if you like.

Pears with Hot Fudge Sauce

Preparation Time 5 minutes • Cooking Time 15 minutes • Serves 4 • Per Serving 301 calories, 16g fat (of which 10g saturates), 40g carbohydrate, 0.4g salt • Vegetarian • Easy

75g (3oz) butter

1 tbsp golden syrup

75g (3oz) light muscovado sugar

4 tbsp evaporated milk or single or double cream

4 ripe pears, cored, sliced and chilled

1. Melt the butter, syrup, sugar and evaporated milk or cream together over a very low heat. Stir thoroughly until all the sugar has dissolved, then bring the fudge mixture to the boil without any further stirring.

2. Put each pear in a serving dish and pour the hot fudge sauce over it. Serve immediately.

Golden Honey Fruits

Preparation Time 5 minutes • Cooking Time 5–8 minutes • Serves 4 • Per Serving 160 calories, trace fat, 40g carbohydrate, 0g salt • Vegetarian • Easy

900g (2lb) selection of tropical fruit, such as pineapple, mango, papaya and banana
3 tbsp runny honey
Greek yogurt to serve
mixed spice to sprinkle

1. Preheat the grill to high. Peel the fruit as necessary and cut into wedges.

2. Put the fruit on to a foil-lined grill pan, drizzle with the honey and cook under the grill for 5–8 minutes until caramelised.

3. Serve with the yogurt, sprinkled with a little mixed spice.

Quick Gooey Chocolate Puddings

Preparation Time 15 minutes • Cooking Time 12–15 minutes • Serves 4 • Per Serving 468 calories,
31g fat (of which 19g saturates), 46g carbohydrate, 0.6g salt • Vegetarian • Easy

**100g (3½oz) unsalted butter, plus
extra to grease**

**100g (3½oz) golden caster sugar,
plus extra to dust**

**100g (3½oz) plain chocolate (at
least 70% cocoa solids), broken
into pieces**

2 large eggs

20g (¾oz) plain flour

icing sugar to dust

1. Preheat the oven to 200°C
(180°C fan oven) mark 6. Butter
four 200ml (7fl oz) ramekins and
dust with sugar. Melt the chocolate
and butter in a heatproof bowl set
over a pan of gently simmering
water, making sure the base of the
bowl doesn't touch the water. Take
the bowl off the pan and leave to
cool for 5 minutes.

2. Whisk the eggs, caster sugar
and flour together in a bowl until
smooth. Fold in the chocolate
mixture and pour into the ramekins.

3. Stand the dishes on a baking tray
and bake for 12–15 minutes until
the puddings are puffed and set on
the outside, but still runny inside.

4. Turn out, dust with icing sugar
and serve immediately.

Mocha Soufflés

Preparation Time 15 minutes, plus cooling • Cooking Time 12 minutes • Serves 6 • Per Serving 132 calories,
5g fat (of which 2g saturates), 20g carbohydrate, 0.2g salt • Vegetarian • Easy

**50g (2oz) plain chocolate (at least
  70% cocoa solids), roughly
  chopped**
1 tbsp cornflour
1 tbsp cocoa powder
1–1½ tsp instant coffee granules
4 tbsp golden caster sugar
150ml (¼ pint) skimmed milk
2 medium egg yolks
3 medium egg whites
icing sugar or cocoa powder to dust

1. Preheat the oven to 190°C
(170°C fan oven) mark 5 and put
a baking sheet inside to heat up.

2. Put the chocolate into a non-
stick pan with the cornflour, cocoa
powder, coffee granules, 1 tbsp
caster sugar and the milk. Warm
gently, stirring over a low heat,
until the chocolate has melted.
Increase the heat and cook,
stirring continuously, until the
mixture just thickens. Leave to
cool a little, then stir in the egg
yolks. Cover the surface with a
piece of damp greaseproof paper
and allow to cool.

3. Put the egg whites into a clean,
grease-free bowl and whisk until
soft peaks form. Gradually whisk
in the remaining caster sugar,
a spoonful at a time, until the
meringue is stiff but not dry.

4. Stir one-third of the meringue
into the cooled chocolate mixture
to lighten it, then gently fold in the
remainder, using a large metal
spoon. Divide the mixture among
six 150ml (¼ pint) ramekins or
ovenproof tea or coffee cups.
Stand them on the hot baking sheet
and bake for about 12 minutes or
until puffed up.

5. Dust the soufflés with a little
icing sugar or cocoa powder and
serve immediately.

Chocolate Crêpes with a Boozy Sauce

Preparation Time 5 minutes, plus standing • Cooking Time 10–15 minutes • Serves 4 • Per Serving 594 calories, 35g fat (of which 17g saturates), 57g carbohydrate, 0.5g salt • Vegetarian • Easy

100g (3½oz) plain flour, sifted

a pinch of salt

1 medium egg

300ml (½ pint) semi-skimmed milk

sunflower oil for frying

50g (2oz) plain chocolate (at least 70% cocoa solids), roughly chopped

100g (3½oz) unsalted butter

100g (3½oz) light muscovado sugar, plus extra to sprinkle

4 tbsp brandy

1. Put the flour and salt into a bowl, make a well in the centre and add the egg. Use a balloon whisk to mix the egg with a little of the flour, then gradually add the milk to make a smooth batter. Cover and leave to stand for about 20 minutes.

2. Pour the batter into a jug. Heat 1 tsp oil in a 23cm (9in) frying pan, then pour in 100ml (3½fl oz) batter, tilting the pan so that the mixture coats the bottom, and fry for 1–2 minutes until golden underneath. Turn carefully and fry the other side. Tip on to a plate, cover with greaseproof paper and repeat with the remaining batter, using more oil as needed.

3. Divide the chocolate among the crêpes. Fold each crêpe in half, and then in half again.

4. Put the butter and sugar into a heavy-based frying pan over a low heat. Add the brandy and stir. Slide the crêpes into the pan and cook for 3–4 minutes to melt the chocolate. Serve drizzled with sauce and sprinkled with sugar.

TRY SOMETHING DIFFERENT

Replace the brandy with Grand Marnier and use orange-flavoured plain chocolate.

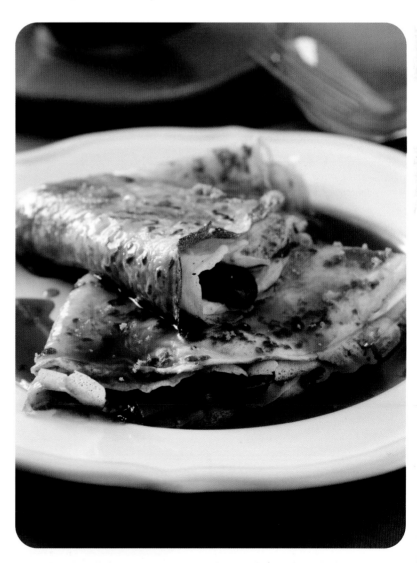

Summer Gratin

Preparation Time 15 minutes • Cooking Time 15 minutes • Serves 4 • Per Serving 168 calories,
4g fat (of which 1g saturates), 27g carbohydrate, 0g salt • Vegetarian • Easy

3 ripe peaches, halved, stoned and sliced
225g (8oz) wild strawberries or raspberries
3 tbsp Kirsch or eau de vie de Mirabelle
4 large egg yolks
50g (2oz) caster sugar

1. Put the peach slices into a bowl with the strawberries or raspberries and 2 tbsp Kirsch or eau de vie.

2. Put the egg yolks, sugar, the remaining Kirsch and 2 tbsp water into a heatproof bowl set over a pan of barely simmering water. Whisk for 5–10 minutes until the mixture leaves a trail when the whisk is lifted, and is warm in the centre. Remove from the heat. Preheat the grill.

3. Arrange the fruit in four shallow heatproof dishes and spoon the sauce over them. Cook under the grill for 1–2 minutes or until light golden. Serve immediately.

TRY SOMETHING DIFFERENT
Use mango slices and blueberries and replace the Kirsch with Cointreau.

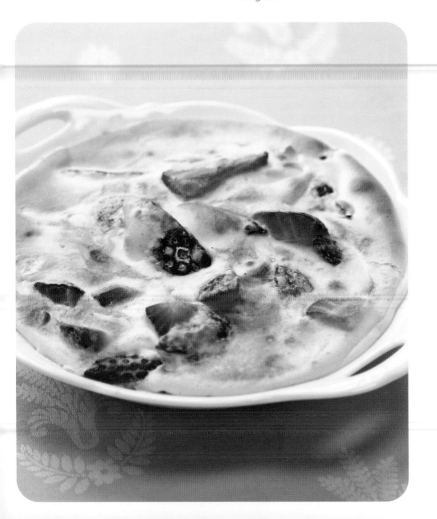

Amaretti with Lemon Mascarpone

Preparation Time 15 minutes • Cooking Time 5 minutes • Serves 4 • Per Serving 180 calories,
8g fat (of which 4g saturates), 28g carbohydrate, 0.4g salt • Vegetarian • Easy

**finely sliced zest and juice of
¼ lemon (see Cook's Tips)
1 tbsp golden caster sugar, plus
a little extra to sprinkle
50g (2oz) mascarpone cheese
12 amaretti biscuits**

1. Put the lemon juice into a small pan. Add the sugar and dissolve over a low heat. Once the sugar has dissolved, add the lemon zest and cook for 1–2 minutes – it will curl up. Using a slotted spoon, lift out the zest strips and lay them on a sheet of baking parchment, reserving the syrup. Sprinkle the strips with sugar to coat.

2. Beat the mascarpone in a bowl to soften, then stir in the reserved sugar syrup.

3. Put a blob of mascarpone on each amaretti biscuit, then top with a couple of strips of the crystallised lemon peel.

COOK'S TIPS

• *To prepare the strips of zest, pare the rind from the lemon, remove any white pith, and finely slice the zest into long strips.*
• *If you're short of time, buy a packet of crystallised lemon slices and use these to decorate the pudding. Alternatively, decorate each biscuit with a little finely grated lemon zest.*

Cheat's Raspberry Ice Cream

Preparation Time 5 minutes • Serves 6 • Per Serving 306 calories, 26g fat (of which 16g saturates), 19g carbohydrate, 0g salt • Vegetarian • Easy

300g (11oz) frozen raspberries
5–6 tbsp golden icing sugar
300ml (½ pint) extra-thick double cream
summer fruit or wafers to serve

1. Put six ramekins or freezerproof glasses into the freezer to chill. Put the frozen raspberries (don't allow them to thaw first) into a food processor with the icing sugar. Whiz for 3–4 seconds until the raspberries look like large crumbs. Add the cream and whiz again for 10 seconds.

2. Spoon into the ice-cold dishes and serve immediately, or spoon into a small freezerproof container and freeze for 20–30 minutes. Serve with summer fruit or wafers, if you like.

COOK'S TIP
Depending on the sweetness of the raspberries, you may need to add a little more icing sugar – taste the mixture before you spoon the ice cream into the dishes.

Cherry Yogurt Crush

Preparation Time 10 minutes, plus chilling • Serves 4 • Per Serving 390 calories, 18g fat (of which 9g saturates), 45g carbohydrate, 0.5g salt • Vegetarian • Easy

400g can stoned cherries, drained, or 450g (1lb) fresh cherries, stoned
500g (1lb 2oz) Greek yogurt
150g (5oz) ratafia biscuits
4 tbsp cherry brandy (optional)

1. Spoon some cherries into the base of each of four 400ml (14fl oz) glasses. Top with a dollop of yogurt, some ratafia biscuits and a drizzle of cherry brandy if you like. Continue layering up each glass until all the ingredients have been used.

2. Chill for 15 minutes–2 hours before serving.

Eton Mess

Preparation Time 10 minutes • Serves 6 • Per Serving 198 calories, 5g fat (of which 3g saturates), 33g carbohydrate, 0.1g salt • Vegetarian • Easy

200g (7oz) fromage frais, chilled
200g (7oz) low-fat Greek yogurt, chilled
1 tbsp golden caster sugar
2 tbsp strawberry liqueur
6 meringues, roughly crushed
350g (12oz) strawberries, hulled and halved

1. Put the fromage frais and yogurt into a large bowl and stir to combine.

2. Add the sugar, strawberry liqueur, meringues and strawberries. Mix together gently and divide among six dishes.

TRY SOMETHING DIFFERENT
Caribbean Crush
Replace the sugar and liqueur with dulce de leche toffee sauce and the strawberries with sliced bananas.

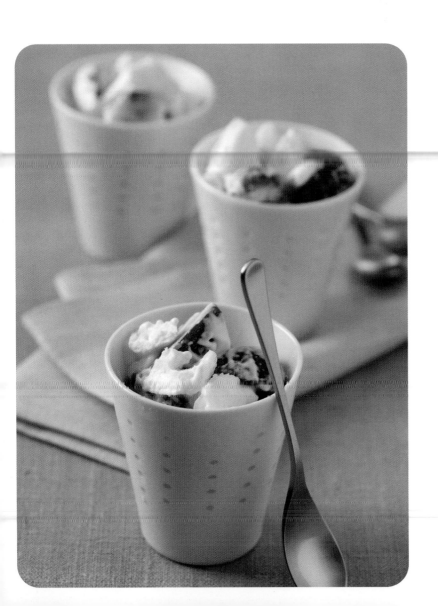

Exotic Fruit Salad

Preparation Time 10 minutes • Serves 4 • Per Serving 187 calories, 1g fat (of which 0g saturates), 47g carbohydrate, 0.1g salt • Vegetarian • Easy

2 oranges
1 mango, peeled, stoned and chopped
450g (1lb) peeled and diced fresh pineapple
200g (7oz) blueberries
½ Charentais melon, cubed
grated zest and juice of 1 lime

1. Using a sharp knife, peel the oranges, remove the pith and cut the flesh into segments. Put into a bowl.

2. Add the mango, pineapple, blueberries and melon to the bowl, then add the lime zest and juice. Gently mix together and serve immediately.

TRY SOMETHING DIFFERENT
• *Use 2 papayas, peeled, seeded and chopped, instead of the pineapple.*
• *Mix the seeds of 2 passion fruit with the lime juice before adding to the salad.*

Tropical Fruit Pots

Preparation Time 15 minutes • Cooking Time 5 minutes • Serves 8 • Per Serving 192 calories,
1g fat (of which trace saturates), 45g carbohydrate, 0.1g salt • Vegetarian • Easy

400g can apricots in fruit juice
2 balls of stem ginger in syrup,
finely chopped, plus 2 tbsp syrup
from the jar
½ tsp ground cinnamon
juice of 1 orange
3 oranges, cut into segments
1 mango, peeled, stoned and
chopped
1 pineapple, peeled, core removed,
and chopped
450g (1lb) coconut yogurt
3 tbsp lemon curd
3–4 tbsp light muscovado sugar

1. Drain the juice from the apricots
into a pan and stir in the syrup from
the ginger. Add the chopped stem
ginger, the cinnamon and orange
juice. Put over a low heat and stir
gently. Bring to the boil, then
reduce the heat and simmer for
2–3 minutes to make a thick syrup.

2. Roughly chop the apricots and
put into a bowl with the segmented
oranges, the mango and pineapple.
Pour the syrup over the fruit. Divide
among eight 300ml (½ pint)
glasses or dessert bowls.

3. Beat the yogurt and lemon curd
together in a bowl until smooth.
Spoon a generous dollop over the
fruit and sprinkle with muscovado
sugar. Chill if not serving
immediately.

GET AHEAD

To prepare ahead *Complete the*
recipe to the end of step 2 up to
2 hours before you plan to eat –
no need to chill.
To use *Complete the recipe.*

Spiced Nectarines

Preparation Time 10 minutes, plus cooling • Serves 4 • Per Serving 95 calories, trace fat, 23g carbohydrate, 0g salt • Vegetarian • Easy

4 tbsp clear honey
2 star anise
1 tbsp lemon juice
4 ripe nectarines or peaches,
   halved and stoned
cream or vanilla ice cream to serve

1. Put the honey, star anise and lemon juice into a heatproof bowl. Stir in 150ml (¼ pint) boiling water and leave until just warm.

2. Add the nectarines or peaches to the warm honey syrup and leave to cool. Serve with cream or vanilla ice cream.

TRY SOMETHING DIFFERENT
Use a cinnamon stick instead of the star anise.

Index